The Back Door
Into My Kitchen

Text copyright ©
2011 by ADmate

Photography copyright ©
2011 by Dana Haddad

Photographs Retouching copyright ©
2011 by ADmate

Operational Director
Nada Harb

All the photographs in this publication were taken by the cook herself on different occasions.

©All rights reserved. No part of this publication may be reproduced or transmitted in any form or by any means, electronic or mechanical, including photocopy or any storage and retrieval system, without written permission from the publisher.

ISBN 978-9953-0-2216-1

First edition 2011

For more information please check:
www.thebackdoorintomykitchen.com

Conceptualized & Designed by admate
www.admate.me

Printed By
Arab Printing Press

To my husband, simple words cannot entirely express my appreciation for your never-ending love, effort and support. You stood by me in creating something very special, as you have always done, and without you this world would have not been possible.

To my children, how can I thank you for your endless encouragements, love and friendship, when I lost faith, you did not, and believed in me to carry on.

To my family, thank you for your knowledge, understanding, dedication, consideration, kindheartedness love, generosity and devotion.

I would like to thank you from the bottom of my heart, but for you my heart has no bottom.

Dana.

Contents

08	Dips and Sauces
22	Salads
48	Pickles, Jams & Chutney
62	Dough
90	Soups
106	Pasta and Rice
150	Vegeterian Dishes
178	Seafood
196	Poultry
210	Meats
260	Dairy Products
270	Sweets

Dips and Sauces

Dips are food's accessory, just like an outfit looks dull without its pearls and ruffles, food doesn't taste good without its dipping that makes it moist and mouthwatering.

Tomato and Avocado Dip

Ingredients:
2 ripe avocados
1 small tomato finely chopped
1 small onion finely chopped
2 tablespoons of lemon juice
2 drops Tabasco sauce
Sprinkle of salt
Sprinkle of white pepper
½ a teaspoon chili powder (optional)

Method:
1. Mash avocados with a fork, add lemon juice and tomato combine well.
2. Stir in the onion, chili sauce and season with salt and pepper.
3. Serve immediately, or place the avocado seed in the middle of the mixture, cover with plastic wrap and refrigerate. Remove seed before serving.

Note: Keep the avocado seeds to maintain the green color

Cucumber Dip

Ingredients:
250g plain yoghurt
2 cloves crushed garlic
3 cucumbers finely chopped
Sprinkle of salt
¼ teaspoon dry mint powder

Method:
1. Mix garlic, salt, cucumbers and yoghurt well in a bowl.
2. Sprinkle dry mint.

Salmon Dip

Ingredients:
100g canned salmon
250g creamy cheese
3 tablespoons cream
1 tablespoon fresh chopped dill
1 small onion finely chopped
2 tablespoons lemon juice
Sprinkle of salt
Sprinkle of pepper

Note:
250g canned Tuna can be used to replace the salmon.

Method:
1. Flake the salmon. Remove bone and skin. Combine with lemon juice and seasonings.
2. In a medium bowl whisk creamy cheese, cream, dill and onion. Fold salmon in and toss well.
3. Cover with plastic wrap and refrigerate for an hour before serving.

Hummus

Ingredients:
500g chickpeas
2 cloves garlic crushed
¼ cup tahini
2 tablespoons yoghurt (optional)
¼ cup lemon juice
5 tablespoons water
1 teaspoon salt
Olive oil

Method:
1. Place chickpeas in a large bowl, cover with water and soak over night. Drain and place in a pan with water to boil until soft.
2. In a food processor place chickpeas, garlic and lemon juice. Process until smooth.
3. Add tahini, water and salt. Process for 10 additional seconds.
4. Spread in a serving plate. Drizzle with olive oil and serve with Lebanese bread.

Note:
A 500g can of processed chickpeas can be used instead.

Cheese Dip 1

Ingredients:
2 tablespoons creamy cheese
1 tablespoon mayonnaise

Method:
Use a spoon to mix cheese and mayonnaise well.

Cheese Dip 2

Ingredients:
2 tablespoons creamy cheese
1 ½ tablespoons sweet chili sauce

Method:
Use a spoon to mix well.

Note:
Add two tablespoons of ketchup; it gives an extra kick.

Onion Dip

Ingredients:
1 pack French onion soup
400g plain yoghurt

Method:
Use a spoon to mix the soup and yoghurt well in a bowl.
Leave to rest for 30 minutes.
Serve with crackers.

Avocado Dip

Ingredients:
3 ripe avocados
2 cloves garlic crushed
¼ cup lemon juice
1 teaspoon olive oil
½ a teaspoon salt

Method:
1. Mash avocados with a fork. Stir lemon juice, garlic and salt. Mix well.
2. Place the mixture in a serving plate and drizzle with olive oil. Serve with Lebanese bread.

Note:
You can use Pita bread or crackers.

Balila

Ingredients:
500g canned chickpeas
2 cloves crushed garlic
½ a teaspoon olive oil
3 tablespoons lemon juice
½ a teaspoon salt
1 teaspoon cumin powder

Method:
1. Place chickpeas with little water and boil until soft and heated.
2. Add garlic, salt, cumin powder, oil and lemon.
Heat for 10 seconds.
3. Place the chickpeas in a serving bowl and drizzle with olive oil. Serve warm.

DIPS & SAUCES

Black Olive Dip

Ingredients:
1 cup deseeded black olives
2 pieces anchovy
4 cloves crushed garlic
5 capers
¼ cup lemon juice
¼ cup olive oil
½ a teaspoon fresh oregano

Method:
1. Place olives, garlic and anchovy in a food processor and process for 10 seconds. Scrap down the sides.
2. Add oil until a paste is formed.
3. Add capers, lemon juice and oregano. Process for 5 seconds with increasing speed. Add oil gradually until a paste is formed.
4. Place in a small bowl and serve with crackers.

Egg and Cheese Dip

Ingredients:
5 boiled eggs grated
4 tablespoons cheddar cheese grated
2 tablespoons mayonnaise
1 tablespoon Tabasco sauce
Sprinkle of salt
Sprinkle of pepper

Method:
In a bowl mix eggs, cheese, mayonnaise, Tabasco sauce. Season to taste.
Place in a bowl, serve with crackers.

Eggplant Dip (Babaganouj)

Ingredients:
3 medium eggplants
2 cloves garlic crushed
¼ cup tahini
¼ cup lemon juice
1 teaspoon olive oil
½ a teaspoon salt
Sprinkle of paprika

Method:
1. Char grill the eggplants until soft. Remove the skin and place the flesh in a medium bowl.
2. Whisk garlic, salt, tahini, lemon juice and water well, fold the eggplant until combined.
3. Place in a serving plate. Drizzle olive oil and sprinkle paprika on top. Serve with Lebanese bread.

Fava Beans (Foul Medamas)

Ingredients:
300g Fava beans (dry)
2 cloves garlic crushed
½ a cup lemon juice
4 tablespoons olive oil
½ a teaspoon salt
½ a teaspoon cumin

Method:
1. Place Fava beans in a bowl, cover with water and soak over night. Drain well, place with water in a medium pan and boil until soft. Drain and keep aside.
2. In a bowl stir in beans, garlic, salt, and about 5 tablespoons of the boiling water. Use a fork or pestle motor to mash the beans.
3. Whisk lemon juice, olive oil and cumin. Add to the beans. Mix well. Pour in a serving plate and drizzle with extra olive oil. Serve with Lebanese bread.

Mouhamara

Ingredients:
8 tablespoons breadcrumbs
(find breadcrumbs)
4 tablespoons chili paste
3 tablespoons pomegranate molasses
1 medium onion grated
5 walnuts
½ a cup water
½ cup lemon juice
4 tablespoons olive oil
½ a teaspoon salt
1 tablespoon sugar
1 teaspoon cumin powder

Note: Serve beside baked kibbé (Ref. pg 250)

Method:
1. In a bowl combine chili paste, lemon juice, molasses, sugar, salt, cumin, oil and water into a paste.
2. Add onion and bread crumbs, combine well to a paste. If too thick, add extra water.
3. Place the mixture in a serving plate with the walnuts on top.

Garlic Dip

Ingredients:
2 bulbs garlic
½ a cup lemon juice
1 to 1½ cups corn oil
1 teaspoon salt

Method:
1. Place garlic and salt in a food processor and process well scraping down the sides.
2. Pour oil in a thin stream while processing until a creamy paste is formed.
3. Place in a bowl. Use for grilled chicken or as spread for sandwiches.

Crab Dip

Ingredients:
2 small cans crabmeat
½ a cup Ricotta cheese
¼ cup thick cream
1 tablespoon fresh chopped dill
3 tablespoons lemon juice
Sprinkle of salt
Sprinkle of pepper

Method:
Place all in a medium bowl and combine well. Serve with toast, Lebanese bread or crackers.

Note: Adding chopped chili while mixing is optional.

Chili Sauce

Ingredients:
1 red capsicum
3 fresh red chilies
3 fresh orange chilies
1 carrot
2 lime juice
2 cloves garlic
1 onion
1/3 cup vinegar
1 teaspoon salt
Pinch of sugar

Method:
1. Process all ingredients in a food processor to a creamy mixture.
2. Add mixture and boil in a large pan. Simmer and occasionally stir until mixture is pulpy. Strain.
3. Return the mixture to boil until it slightly thickens. Pour into clean warm bottles. Seal when cold.

Dan's Sauce

Ingredients:
2 garlic cloves crushed
1 tablespoon fresh basil chopped
1 tablespoon mustard
1 tablespoon ketchup
¼ cup vinegar
4 tablespoons olive oil
1 tablespoon salt

Method:
Place all ingredients in a medium jar. Shake well and use as dressing for salads or grilled chicken

Ketchup

Ingredients:
10 medium ripe tomatoes
¼ to ½ a cup of sugar
2 cups water
1 tablespoon tomato paste
1 tablespoon mustard powder
¾ cup vinegar
2 bay leaves
1 cinnamon stick
2 cloves

Method:
1. Place bay leaves, cloves and cinnamon in a small fine cloth. Close tightly.
2. Combine water, sugar, chopped tomatoes, mustard, tomato paste and the cloth. Bring to boil for 10 minutes. Simmer until tomatoes are pulpy.
3. Add vinegar. Stir until the mixture thickens. Process until smooth and creamy. Pour into clean jars or bottles. Seal when cold.

Hint: Add red chilli for extra kick

Sweet Chili Sauce

Ingredients:
6 large red chilies
1 cup sugar
½ a cup water
2 tablespoons fresh coriander
2 tablespoons rice vinegar
½ aa tablespoon corn flour

Method:
1. Combine sugar and water. Bring to boil. Stir in chopped chilies, coriander and simmer for 10 minutes.
2. Add vinegar and simmer for 3minutes. Remove from heat. Process until smooth and place back in pan.
3. Stir in blended corn flour and extra water stirring until the mixture thickens. Pour into clean warm bottles or jars. Seal when cool.

D.H. Sauce

Ingredients:
1 kg chopped tomatoes
4 chopped apples
13 chopped onions
1 cup chopped dates
5 cups raisins
3 cups vinegar
1 teaspoon mixed spice
1 teaspoon mustard seeds
1 small fresh chili
2 cups sugar

Method:
1. Combine all in a large pan except sugar; simmer until mixture is pulpy.
2. Place all in a processor until smooth.
3. Drain mixture in a sieve and return to pan. Stir in sugar and bring to boil; keep stirring until sauce thickens.
4. Pour into clean warm bottles. Seal when cold.
5. Use for steak or chicken.

Sweet and Sour Sauce

Ingredients:
1 cup pineapple juice
½ a cup water
1/3 cup vinegar
2 tablespoons ketchup
2 tablespoons Worcestershire sauce
4 tablespoons soy sauce
2 ½ tablespoons corn flour or potato flour
1/3 cup sugar
½ a teaspoon salt

Method:
1. Combine all ingredients in a medium pan.
2. Bring to boil stirring until sauce thickens.
3. Pour into bottles or jars; seal when cold.

Salads

What is more refreshing than salads when your appetite seems to have deserted you, or even after a capacious dinner - the nice, fresh, green, and crisp salad, full of life and health. A good salad is full with hope that natural food can taste heavenly.

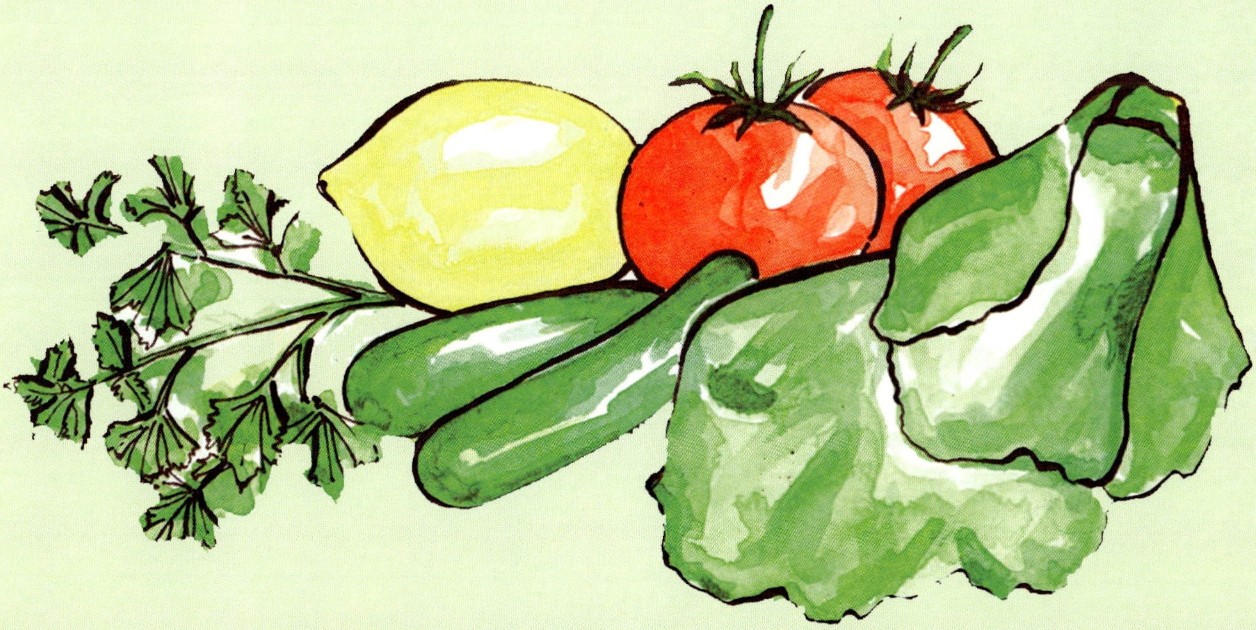

Grilled Salad

Ingredients:
2 eggplants
2 zucchinis
400g fresh mushrooms
500g sweet potatos
4 tablespoons olive oil

Dressing:

2 cloves crushed garlic
¼ cup fresh basil leaves
¼ cup olive oil
4 tablespoons balsamic vinegar
¼ teaspoon sugar
Sprinkle of salt

Method:
1. Cut the potatoes and eggplants to thick slices and slice zucchinis length way.
2. Brush the vegetables with oil and char grill until lightly browned and soft. Place in a separate plate.
3. In a food processor place garlic, oil, vinegar, sugar and basil leaves until well processed.
4. Mix the vegetables with the dressing very well and serve

Note: Other vegetables of your liking can be added.

Green Salad

Ingredients:
1 whole lettuce
5 tablespoons olive oil
¼ cup lemon juice
or 5 tablespoons apple vinegar
½ a teaspoon salt

Method:
1. Tear the lettuce into pieces and put in a large serving bowl.
2. Combine vinegar or lemon juice, oil and salt in a small screw-top jar. Seal the jar and shake well.
3. Pour the sauce over the lettuce and toss well before serving.

Country Slaw

Ingredients:
1 cup mayonnaise
3 tablespoons lemon juice
4 cups finely shredded cabbage
1 cup grated carrots
½ a green capsicum cut into fine strips (optional)
1 teaspoon salt
2 tablespoons sugar

Method:
1. In a big bowl mix cabbage, carrots and capsicum.
2. Add mayonnaise, lemon juice, sugar and salt.
Mix until the cabbage becomes well coated with dressing.

Rocket Salad with Vegetables

Ingredients:
150g eggplant or zucchini
200g rocket leaves
2 tablespoons grated parmesan
4 tablespoons balsamic vinegar
4 tablespoons olive oil
2 tablespoons lemon juice
¼ cup olive oil extra
Sprinkle of salt

Method:
1. Cut eggplants or zucchinis to small cubes heat oil extra in a frying pan. Stir and cook until the eggplants/zucchinis are golden in color. Remove from heat, and drain on absorbent paper.
2. In a medium bowl, mix vinegar, oil, lemon juice and salt. Stir in the eggplants/zucchinis and place the rocket leaves on top. Sprinkle the parmesan and serve.

Onion Salad

Ingredients:
200g white onions
100g rocket leaves
1 cup shaved parmesan
4 tablespoons lemon juice
¼ cup olive oil
½ a teaspoon salt
½ a teaspoon black pepper

Method:
1. Cut the onions into medium-thick slices, brush with olive oil on both sides and bake in a hot oven until golden in color.
2. Remove from oven and sprinkle salt and pepper. Place on a plate and drizzle with olive oil and lemon juice.
3. Tear the rocket leaves into pieces and place over the onions with shaved parmesan.

Cabbage Salad

Ingredients:
300g sliced cabbage
2 garlic cloves crushed
3 medium tomatoes chopped (optional)
½ a cup lemon juice
6 tablespoons olive oil
½ a teaspoon salt

Method:
1. Combine garlic, lemon juice, olive oil and salt in a small screw-top jar. Seal the jar and shake well.
2. In a big bowl place the cabbage and mix well with the dressing. Wait for 5 minutes before serving.

Tomato Salad

Ingredients:
500g finely chopped red tomatoes
1 finely chopped spring onion
1 finely chopped green chili (optional)
¼ cup olive oil
½ a teaspoon salt

Method:
1. In a medium bowl place the tomatoes, onion and chili. Mix well.
2. Stir the olive oil and salt mixing well. Serve with Lebanese bread.

Yoghurt Salad

Ingredients:
2 cups yoghurt or fruit yoghurt
1 garlic clove crushed
1 finely chopped tomato
3 finely chopped cucumbers
Sprinkle of salt
1 teaspoon dry mint powder

Method:
1. In a big bowl place the yoghurt, garlic and salt. Mix well.
2. Add the cucumbers and the tomatoes and stir well. Sprinkle the dry mint.

Note: Add any vegetable of your choice.

Beetroot Salad (Shamandar)

Ingredients:
500g fresh beetroot
1 garlic clove crushed
¼ cup lemon juice
3 tablespoons olive oil
Sprinkle of salt

Method:
1. In a medium pan, place the beetroot with water and bring to boil until tender. Remove from heat and leave to cool. Peel and slice.
2. In a bowl, stir the garlic, salt, lemon juice and olive oil. Add beetroot, toss well and serve.

Note: Add 2 cups finely sliced cabbage mix with beetroot.

Mum slaw

Ingredients:
6 cups finely sliced cabbage
1 grated carrot
2 garlic cloves crushed
¼ cup lemon juice
1 cup mayonnaise
¼ cup milk
6 tablespoon olive oil
¼ teaspoon salt

Method:
1. In a big bowl stir in the garlic, lemon juice, salt, mayonnaise, milk and olive oil mix well.
2. Add cabbage and carrot mix and toss well. Wait for 5 minutes before serving.

Pine Nut Salad

Ingredients:
1 medium lettuce
¼ cup pine nuts
1 cup corn kernel
1 garlic clove crushed
½ a cup lemon or lime juice
5 tablespoons olive oil
½ a tablespoon Dijon mustard
Sprinkle of salt
1 teaspoon herbes de Provence
Sprinkle of black pepper
½ a teaspoon dry basil powder

Method:
1. In a medium frying pan, toast the pine nuts stirring frequently until golden in color.
2. In a medium bowl, whisk the oil garlic, basil, herbes de Provence, mustard, salt, pepper, lemon juice and pine nuts. Let stand for 1 hour.
3. In a serving bowl tear the lettuce into pieces. Add the corn, stir the dressing and serve.

Tuna Macaroni Salad

Ingredients:
400g small pasta
2 cans tuna shredded with oil
1 cup finely chopped mixed pickles
3 tablespoons mustard
4 tablespoons white vinegar
½ a cup mayonnaise
1 teaspoon lemon juice
Sprinkle of salt

Method:
1. Boil water in a medium pan, place pasta and cook until tender. Remove from heat and drain in a colander.
2. In a large serving bowl, stir in tuna, pickles, mustard, vinegar, salt, mayonnaise and lemon juice. Mix well.
3. Add pasta, mix well and cover with plastic wrap. Keep for 20 minutes in refrigerator before serving.

Potato Salad

Ingredients:
1 kg unpeeled baby potatoes
1 tablespoon chopped fresh parsley
1 garlic clove crushed
3 tablespoons olive oil
5 tablespoons lemon juice
Sprinkle of salt

Method:
1. Place the potatoes in a large pan of cold salted water and bring to boil until tender. Peel and cut into cubes. Drain well and place in a large bowl.
2. In a medium bowl, whisk the garlic, olive oil, salt and lemon juice. Stir the potato and toss well to coat with the dressing. Sprinkle parsley and serve.

Pasta Salad

Ingredients:
500g small pasta cooked
2 garlic cloves crushed
1 cup corn kernel
150g canned chopped artichokes
100g sliced mushrooms
2 finely chopped cucumbers
1 finely chopped tomato
200g sliced lettuce
1 ½ tablespoons mustard
½ a cup mayonnaise
2 tablespoons olive oil
2 tablespoons lemon juice
Sprinkle of salt

Method:
1. In a large serving bowl, whisk the garlic, mustard, mayonnaise, lemon juice, olive oil and salt while very well mixing.
2. Add corn, artichokes, mushrooms, cucumbers, tomato and lettuce and toss well.
3. Stir in the pasta and toss well. Cover with a plastic wrap and keep in the refrigerator for 20 minutes before serving.

Avocado Salad

Ingredients:
2 medium chopped avocados
2 chopped spring onions
1 tablespoon chopped fresh parsley
½ a cup chopped pineapple
½ a crushed clove garlic
4 tablespoons mayonnaise
2 tablespoons ketchup (optional)
4 tablespoons lemon juice
Sprinkle of salt
Sprinkle of chili powder (optional)

Method:
1. In a large serving bowl, whisk the mayonnaise, garlic, salt and lemon juice well.
2. Add the onions, pineapples and avocado. Toss well and sprinkle the parsley.

Note: For additional flavor chop 1 green apple and 1 cup of small boiled prawn and add to the mix.

Dan's salad Sauce

Ingredients:
2 garlic cloves crushed (creamy)
5 fresh basil leaves chopped
3 tablespoons mustard
4 tablespoons ketchup
¼ cup apple vinegar
5 tablespoons olive oil

Method:
Place all ingredients in a medium jar. Shake well and use as dressing for salads.

Broad Bean Salad

Ingredients:
2 cups broad beans
1 garlic clove crushed
¼ cup olive oil
¼ cup lemon juice
1 tablespoon fresh chopped parsley
Sprinkle of salt

Method:
1. Place the beans in a large bowl and cover with water over night.
2. Drain and place in a medium pan with water. Boil until tender then remove from heat and drain.
3. Whisk the oil, lemon juice, salt, and garlic, add the beans, toss well and sprinkle the parsley.

Nad Salad

Ingredients:
1 packet instant noodles with seasoning
4 cups finely sliced cabbage
1 green capsicum cut into fine strips
½ a cup olive oil
½ a cup apple vinegar
¼ cup sugar

Method:
1. In a medium serving bowl, place the noodles and crush them. Stir the seasonings over.
2. Mix the cabbage and the capsicum with the noodles.
3. Whisk oil, vinegar and sugar in a small bowl and pour over the noodles. Mix well, and wait 10 minutes before serving.

Feta Salad

Ingredients:
200g cubed feta cheese
4 chopped red tomatoes
1 chopped green capsicum
2 chopped cucumbers
¼ cup deseeded black olives
4 tablespoons olive oil
3 tablespoons lemon juice
½ a teaspoon salt
½ a teaspoon herbes de Provence

Method:
1. In a large serving bowl whisk the oil, herbes de Provence, lemon juice and salt.
2. Add olives, cucumber, capsicum, tomatoes and cheese. Toss well and serve.

Hal Salad

Ingredients:
1 can tuna
1 teaspoon mustard
Sprinkle of salt
150g kernel corn
2 sliced cucumbers
½ a cup lemon juice
4 tablespoons olive oil

Method:
1. In a serving bowl whisk the lemon juice, mustard, salt and oil well.
2. Add tuna, corn and cucumbers and toss well. Serve with toast bread.

Rocket Leaf Salad

Ingredients:
500g fresh rocket leaves
1 garlic clove crushed
6 tablespoons olive oil
4 tablespoons vinegar
½ a teaspoon salt
Sprinkle of white pepper

Method:
1. In a small bowl, whisk garlic, salt, pepper, oil and vinegar to mix well.
2. In a serving bowl, tear the rocket leaves into pieces or leave as whole. Stir the dressing and toss the whole well.

Squid Salad

Ingredients:
500g fresh or frozen squids
2 chopped red tomatoes
2 cups rocket leaves
1 garlic clove crushed
1 zucchini
¼ cup olive oil
4 tablespoons lemon juice
Pinch of salt
Pinch of Cayenne pepper

Method:
1. Cut the squid to thick rings, place in a frying pan with 1 tablespoon of oil and heat for 2 minutes until tender. Remove from heat and drain. Place on absorbent paper.
2. Whisk the oil, lemon juice, garlic, salt and Cayenne. Toss the squids in the dressing and keep marinated for 10 minutes.
3. Use a swivel-bladed vegetable peeler to cut the zucchini to long ribbons. Mix with rockets leaves, tomatoes and the coated calamari to serve.

Papaya Salad

Ingredients:
1 medium green papaya
1 medium lettuce
1 finely chopped red chili
¼ cup roasted peanuts
¼ cup lemon juice
2 tablespoons fish sauce
3 teaspoons sugar

Method:
1. Shred the lettuce on a serving plate, top with grated papaya.
2. Whisk the lemon juice, fish sauce, sugar and chili. Pour over the salad and sprinkle the roasted peanuts on top.

Fattoush

Ingredients:
1 chopped capsicum
4 tomatoes sliced into chunks
4 cucumbers sliced into chunks
2 sliced spring onions
2 garlic cloves crushed
1 cup fresh parsley leaves
1 cup fresh mint leaves
½ a bunch watercress
1 whole lettuce sliced
4 small sliced parsnips
½ a cup olive oil
4 loaves toasted Lebanese bread
1 teaspoon salt
½ a teaspoon black pepper
1 tablespoon sumac (red sour powder)

Method:
1. In a large bowl, stir in all the vegetables and mix well.
2. Combine all the dressing in a small screw top jar. Seal the jar and shake well. Pour over the vegetables and toss well.
3. Crush the toasted bread and sprinkle over the salad to serve.

Warm Tabbouleh

Ingredients:
2 bunches fresh flat leaf parsley chopped
10 fresh mint leaves chopped
5 finely chopped small onions
5 finely chopped red tomatoes
¾ cup burghul (cracked wheat)
1 tablespoon tomato paste
½ a tablespoon chili paste
½ a cup water
½ a cup lemon juice
½ a cup olive oil
¼ teaspoon salt
¼ teaspoon black pepper

Method:
1. Heat oil in a large pan. Add the onions and cook until soft. Stir in the tomato paste, chili paste and lemon juice. Mix well. Add the water and burghul, stirring occasionally until burghul is cooked. Remove from heat.
2. In a big serving bowl place the parsley, mint, tomatoes, lemon juice, salt and pepper. Mix well. Stir in the burghul and serve with boiled cabbage leaves.

Tabbouleh

Ingredients:
2 bunches fresh finely chopped flat leaf parsley
10 fresh mint leaves finely chopped
1 small onion finely chopped
8 tomatoes finely chopped
3 tablespoons of burghul (cracked wheat)
½ a cup lemon juice
¼ cup olive oil
1 teaspoon salt
¼ teaspoon black pepper

Method:
1. Place the burghul in a bowl. Mix with the tomatoes and set aside for 10 minutes.
2. Add parsley, mint and onions to the burghul and mix well.
3. Whisk the oil, lemon juice, salt and pepper together and add to the burghul. Mix gently then cover and chill for 10 minutes before serving.

Rice Salad

Ingredients:
2 cups cold boiled rice
100g fresh small prawns
1 red chili finely sliced
1 chopped onion
½ a ripe pineapple
1 spring onion finely chopped
2 crushed cloves garlic
¼ cup olive oil
1 tablespoon fish sauce

Method:
1. Chop pineapple into small pieces and set aside.
2. Heat half of the oil in a large pan. Add garlic, onion and chili. Cook for 1 minute. Add prawns, stir well and remove all ingredients from the pan and set aside.
3. Reheat the pan and fry the pineapple until lightly golden in color then remove from pan.
4. Add the remaining oil. Place the rice and toss for 3 minutes. Place back the prawns mix with the pineapple and stir well.
5. Remove from heat and add fish sauce. Toss well and place all on the serving plate. Scatter the spring onion over the top and serve.

Oregano Salad

Ingredients:
500g fresh thyme leaves
2 finely chopped onions
1 crushed clove garlic
6 tablespoons olive oil
¼ cup lemon juice
Sprinkle of salt
Sprinkle of white pepper

Method:
1. Combine salt, pepper, oil and lemon juice in a small bowl.
2. Place oregano leaves on a serving plate. Spread the chopped onions on top. Pour over the dressing serve with Lebanese bread.

Silver Beet Salad

Ingredients:
600g fresh silver beet leaves
1 crushed clove garlic
1 cup thick plain yoghurt
½ a cup yoghurt cheese (Labneh)
4 tablespoons olive oil

Method:
1. Finely slice the silver beet leaves and place them in a pan. Heat oil. Add garlic and stir for a minute. Remove from heat to cool.
2. In a large bowl mix the 2 yoghurt types with the leaves and serve.

Green Beans Salad

Ingredients:
500g boiled green beans
1 crushed clove garlic
¼ cup olive oil
1/3 cup lemon juice
Sprinkle of salt
Sprinkle of white pepper

Method:
1. Combine oil, lemon juice, garlic, salt and pepper. Mix well.
2. Place the boiled green beans on a serving plate. Drizzle the dressing on top.

Dandelions (Hindbeh)

Ingredients:
3 onions finely sliced
500g fresh dandelions
2 cloves garlic crushed
½ a cup lemon juice
¼ cup olive oil
¼ teaspoon white pepper
1 teaspoon salt

Method:
1. Place dandelions in a large pan, cover with water and boil well until tender. Drain well and squeeze the water out.
2. In a medium pan, heat the oil. Add the garlic and cook until lightly browned then remove from heat.
3. Add dandelions and cook stirring frequently until almost dry. Season well add lemon juice and toss well.
4. Fry the onion until lightly crisp then drain on absorbent paper.
5. Place dandelions on a serving plate, scatter the crisp onion on top with lemon wedges on the side.

Egg Salad

Ingredients:
1 can corn kernel
1 ½ cups frozen peas boiled
1 canned mushroom
½ cup pickled cucumbers chopped
5 boiled eggs
1 cup mayonnaise
Salt and pepper to season

Method:
1. Combine corn, peas, mushroom, and pickles in a large serving bowl.
2. Whisk mayonnaise, season and stir the vegetables and toss well.
3. Chop the boiled eggs and mix gently in the mayonnaise mixture. Cover with plastic wrap and keep in fridge for 20 minutes before serving.

Halloumi Salad

Ingredients:
300g Halloumi sliced
4 small eggplants
4 tomatoes sliced to thick rounds
300g watercress or rocket leaves
8 fresh basil leaves
4 tablespoons apple vinegar
4 tablespoons olive oil
½ a teaspoon salt
Sprinkle of pepper

Method:
1. Peel and slice eggplants. Coat with flour. Heat oil in a frying pan. Fry the eggplants until golden in color then remove from heat and drain on absorbent paper.
2. In the same frying pan, add sliced Halloumi and fry until lightly golden. Remove from heat and place on a plate.
3. Add tomatoes to the pan for 10 seconds, then remove and place in a plate.
4. In the same pan, without heat, stir vinegar, salt and pepper. Mix well.
5. In a serving plate place the eggplants topped with cheese then tomatoes. Scatter watercress and basil on top and drizzle the dressing from the pan and serve.

Raheb

Ingredients:
3 large eggplants
2 fresh tomatoes
1 green capsicum
2 small white onions
1 clove garlic
2 green chilies
½ a cup lemon juice
½ a cup olive oil
Salt and pepper for seasoning

Method:
1. Char grill capsicum skin side down until skin blackens and blisters, place in a plastic bag and leave to cool. Peel away the skin and chop it.
2. Char grill the eggplants until soft. Use a spoon to scoop the flesh into a bowl with capsicum.
3. Char grill tomatoes, onions, chili and garlic. Peel away the skin and chop them all.
4. In a large bowl whisk lemon juice, salt and oil well. Combine the char grilled vegetables with the dressing, place in a serving plate and drizzle with olive oil.

Note: You can only char grill the eggplant and add the rest of vegetables raw and toss well

Basic Sauce for Pickles

Ingredients:
Green chili (optional)
¼ cup vinegar
4 cups water
¼ cup salt
2 tablespoons sugar

Method:
In a small pan, stir in water, salt, sugar; add vinegar and mix well.

Cucumber Pickles:
Cut small slits in the firm cucumber. Place in a large jar. Pour the sauce. Close the lid firmly. Use in a week time.

Capsicum Pickles:
Same procedure as cucumber pickles.

Sea Weed Pickles:
Same procedure as cucumber pickles. Or only with vinegar.

Cauliflower Pickles:
Same procedure as cucumber pickles.

Mixed Vegetables:
Cut all the vegetables to a medium size and apply the same procedure as for cucumber pickles.

Turnip Pickles:
Slice them with 1 beetroot. Mix all together. Place them in a jar, pour the sauce over. Seal well.

Carrot Pickles:
Slice them and apply the same procedure as for cucumber pickles.

Eggplant Pickles:
1. Use a small size eggplant. Remove the cap only.
2. Boil for 5 minutes. Remove with a slotted spoon. Place on a towel to drain.
3. Cut a slit in each piece and stuff it with crushed garlic, chili and salt. Place them in jar, pour sauce over and use within two weeks.

Eggplant Makdouse:
1. Same procedure as above.
2. Crush garlic, chili, salt, walnuts and mix well. Place them in a slit. Press them in the jar on top of each other. Add olive oil and seal very well. Use within 3 weeks.

Green Olives Pickles:
1. Soak the olives in water for 12 hours.
2. Cut a slit in each. Place them in layers with lemon slices and chili slices in a jar.
3. Mix 10 cups of water with 1 cup of salt. Pour over the olives. Drizzle top with olive oil and seal well.

Black Olives Pickles:
1. Soak in water for 3 hours. Remove the water. Sprinkle olives with salt and stir well.
2. Place them in a jar. Pour olive oil and water to cover. Seal well.

Chili Pickles:
1. Chop the chilies. Leave them aside.
2. Boil water in a pan. Add the chilies to the water.
3. Stir for 10 seconds. Remove them with a slotted spoon and place them in the jar.
4. Pour ¼ cup of sugar and white vinegar. Close tightly and shake well.
5. Serve after an hour.

Orange Marmalade

Ingredients:
1.5 kg oranges
8 cups water
8 cups sugar

Method:
1. Finely slice unpeeled oranges. Combine with water in a bowl for 12 hours.
2. Change the water several times.
3. Place orange mixture in a large pan and bring to boil. Simmer until rind is soft.
4. Add sugar. Stir over heat until sugar dissolves. Boil for 10 to 15 minutes until slightly thick.
5. Pour into clean warm jars. Seal when the mixture cools down.

Strawberry Jam

Ingredients:
1 kg fresh strawberries
4 cups sugar

Method:
1. Combine and mix strawberries and sugar in a large bowl. Refrigerate overnight.
2. Use a slotted spoon to remove the strawberries.
3. Place the syrup in a pan and boil for 15 minutes. Add the strawberries, stirring often. Skim any scum off the surface.
4. Boil for 10 minutes on low heat. Remove from heat and spoon immediately into clean warm jars.
5. Seal the jars and turn them upside down for 5 minutes, then invert and leave to cool.

Note: Use the same steps for Raspberry jam.

Fig Jam

Ingredients:
2.4 kg dried figs
6 cups sugar
1½ cups water
¼ cup anise seeds
¼ cup toasted sesame seeds
½ a cup toasted whole almonds or walnut
1/3 teaspoon crushed Arabic gum with little sugar

Method:
1. Place chopped figs, sugar and water in a large pan. Bring to boil for 20 minutes until soft.
2. Add lemon juice, anise seeds, sesame seeds and almonds. Boil for 20 minutes and remove any scum with slotted spoon.
3. When thick and pulpy, add Arabic gum. Stir for a minute. Pour into clean jars. Cool and seal well.

Apricot Jam

Ingredients:
1 kg fresh apricots
6 cups sugar

Method:
1. Discard seeds from apricots and chop roughly.
2. Stir apricots in a medium pan on low heat until thick. Stir constantly.
3. Add sugar. Stir on low heat until it dissolves. Bring to boil for 15 minutes until thick and golden.
4. Pour into warm clean jars and seal. Turn jars upside down for 3minutes then invert and leave to cool.

Apple Jam

Ingredients:
1 kg finely chopped fresh apples
5 cups sugar
1 tablespoon lemon juice
1 whole clove (optional)
1 crushed Arabic gum

Method:
1. Combine apple and sugar in a large pan. Leave to rest for 1 hour.
2. Place pan over heat. Simmer for 40 minutes stirring frequently until thick. Add crushed Arabic gum with ½ a teaspoon of sugar and stir well.
3. Pour into warm jars and seal when the mixture cools down.

Quince Jam

Ingredients:
1.5 kg quinces
4 cups sugar
4 cups water
4 whole cloves

Method:
1. Peel and discard cores. Chop into small pieces. Combine with the cloves and water in a large pan. Bring to boil until soft.
2. Stir in sugar until it dissolves. Boil for 20 minutes. Pour into warm jars and seal when cool.

Quince Jelly

Ingredients:
1.5 kg quinces
2 cups sugar
4 cups water
4 tablespoons lemon juice

Method:
1. Roughly cut quinces with skin and cores. Combine with water in a large pan. Bring to boil until tender and mash with potato masher.
2. Pour water over muslin bag. Squeeze well. Spoon the quince into the bag and close far away from fruit. Hand over a bowl and allow the mixture to drip overnight.
3. Place the liquid in a large pan. Stir in lemon juice. Add sugar. Stir over low heat until sugar dissolves. Boil for 20 minutes.
4. Remove any scum with a slotted spoon.
5. Pour in warm jars and seal. Turn upside down for 5 minutes then invert and leave to cool.

Fruity Jam

Ingredients:
1 chopped medium pineapple
3 chopped bananas
2 chopped pears
5 chopped apples
1 ¼ cup orange juice
2 tablespoons lemon juice
5 cups sugar

Method:
1. Peel all the fruits. Combine with juices in a large pan. Bring to boil and simmer until fruits are soft.
2. Add sugar. Dissolve and boil uncovered until jam jells when tested.
3. Pour into clean warm jars. Seal when cold.

Cherry Jam

Ingredients:
1 kg fresh cherries
500g sugar
2 tablespoons lemon juice

Method:
1. Remove stalks and pipes from cherry. Place in large pan with 2 cups of water. Bring to boil. Reduce heat and simmer for 10 minutes.
2. Remove cherries with a slotted spoon and keep aside. Add sugar and lemon juice. Boil for 15 minutes and remove any scum.
3. Add cherries and boil for 5 to 10 minutes. Spoon into clean warm jars and seal. Turn jars upside down for 5 minutes then invert and leave to cool.

Apple Jelly

Ingredients:
1 kg apples
5 cups water
3 cups sugar
1 tablespoon lemon juice

Method:
1. Chop apples. Combine with water and boil until soft. Strain mixture through a fine cloth. Allow liquid to drip slowly over night in a bowl.
2. To each cup of liquid, add ¾ cups of sugar. Bring to boil until jelly sets and thickens. Add lemon juice and simmer for 5 minutes.
3. Pour into clean warm jars. Seal when cold.

Onion Marmalade

Ingredients:
½ a kg baby onions
3 tablespoons balsamic vinegar
1 tablespoon olive oil
1/3 cup water
3 tablespoons brown sugar

Method:
1. Heat oil in a medium saucepan. Stir onions until lightly browned.
2. Add sugar, water and stir until dissolved and onions lightly soften. Add vinegar and simmer for 5 minutes
3. Pour into warm jars. Seal when cold.

Nad's Chutney

Ingredients:
1 ½ kg finely chopped tomatoes
5 finely chopped peeled apples
2 finely chopped onions
3 cloves crushed garlic
1 cup vinegar
1 cup black raisins
1 cup sugar
½ a teaspoon mustard powder
1 teaspoon curry powder
1 teaspoon mixed spices
Sprinkle of chili powder

Method:
1. Combine all ingredients in a large pan.
2. Bring to boil, stirring occasionally for and hour and a half until thick. Pour into clean warm jars. Seal when cold.

Apricot Chutney

Ingredients:
4 finely chopped peeled apples
700g chopped Apricots
2 finely chopped onions
1 cup vinegar
1 teaspoon fresh grated ginger
1 cup sugar
1 teaspoon mustard powder
1 clove crushed garlic
Pinch of ground coriander

Method:
Combine all ingredients in a large pan. Bring to boil, stirring occasionally for an hour until mixture is thick. Pour into clean warm jars. Seal when cold.

Sweet Chutney

Ingredients:
200g chopped mixed glace fruit
1 teaspoon corn flour
1 ½ cups water
2 tablespoons honey
1 tablespoon mustard seed
Pinch of ground cloves
1 tablespoon lemon juice
Pinch of ground cinnamon
Pinch of ground nutmeg

Method:
1. Combine water, honey, spices and mustard seeds. Bring to boil.
2. Mix corn flour with little water and add to the mixture stirring until thick.
3. Add mixed glace fruit and lemon juice. Simmer until fruit is soft and thick.
4. Pour into warm clean jars. Seal and leave to cool.

Note: Serve with cold cuts.

Apple Mint Chutney

Ingredients:
5 large peeled and chopped apples
2 chopped onions
½ a cup chopped fresh mint
½ a cup raisins
½ a cup vinegar
1 cup water
½ a cup sugar

Method:
Combine all ingredients in a large pan. Bring to boil stirring occasionally until mixture is thick. Pour into warm jars. Seal when cold.

Dough

Good bread is the great need in poor homes, and oftentimes the best appreciated luxury in the homes of the very rich, it's a universal language, that everyone is entitled to, with no discrimination.

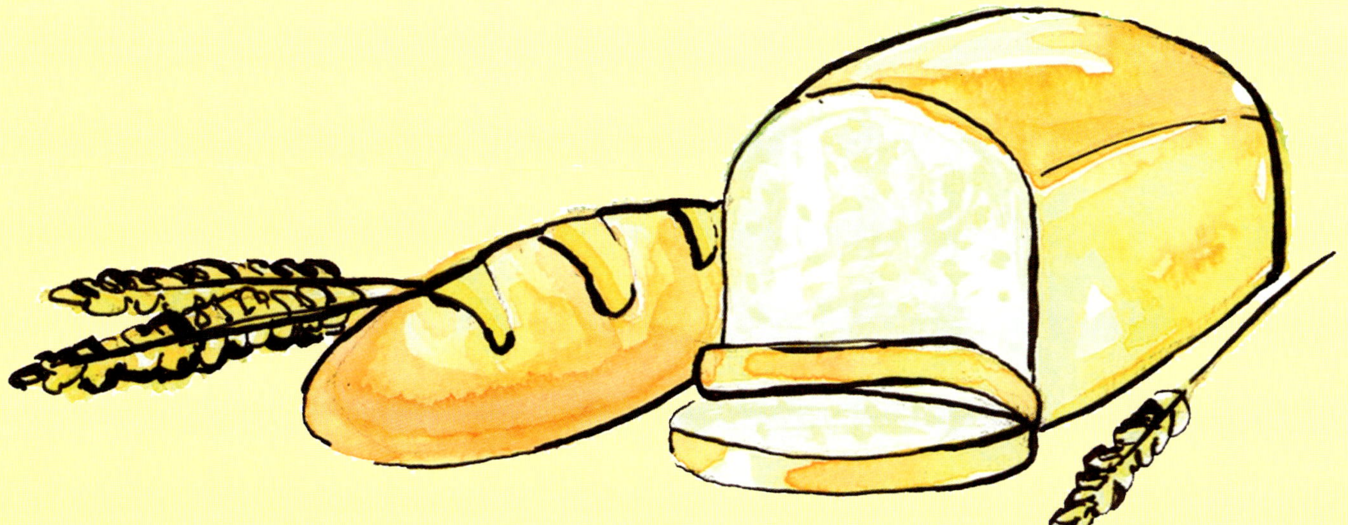

Basic Pizza Dough

Ingredients:
3 cups plain flour
1 ½ cups water
2 tablespoons oil
Sprinkle of sugar and salt
1 teaspoon instant yeast

Method:
1. Combine all the ingredients in large bowl. Mix to a soft non-sticky dough.
2. Turn dough on to floured surface and knead until smooth and elastic. Place in a lightly oiled medium bowl. Cover and keep warm until doubled in size.
3. Flatten 2 pieces of dough to fit a pizza pan. Spread sauce over, topped with fillings.

Basic Sauce:

Ingredients:
4 red tomatoes
1 chopped onion
4 cloves chopped garlic
1 tablespoon olive oil
1 teaspoon dried oregano or basil
Salt and black pepper to season

Method:
1. Heat oil in a saucepan, cook onion and garlic until golden. Add tomatoes, oregano, sugar and seasonings.
2. Bring to boil. Stir occasionally until the sauce thickens. Remove from heat, and keep aside to cool. Place the sauce in a blender and mix to a smooth paste. Spread on dough.

Pizza Toppings:

1. 200g sliced fresh mushroom
1 capsicum
Seeded black olives
2 cups grated Mozzarella cheese
1 cup grated cheddar cheese
Sprinkle of oregano powder
Drizzle olive oil

2. 2 large eggplants sliced and fried
2 finely chopped green chilies
1 cup grated cheddar cheese

3. 20g thinly sliced pepperoni or tuna
100g sliced fresh mushrooms
½ a cup chopped pineapple
1 cup grated Swiss cheese

4. Tomato sauce on base
½ a cup cheddar cheese grated
½ a cup grated Ementhal cheese
Sprinkle of oregano powder

Fatair Sabanekh (Spinach)

Dough:

Ingredients:
1½ cups plain flour
2 tablespoons oil
½ a cup water
½ a teaspoon instant yeast

Method:
1. Combine all in a bowl. Mix to a firm dough. Knead dough on floured surface until smooth then place in a lightly oiled bowl to double in size.
2. Roll pastry to a thin sheet and cut into fluted circles. Add 1 teaspon spinach mixture on the center of each circle. Form the pastries into 3 cornered hat shapes and pinch the edges to seal.
3. Place them in a greased oven tray and bake in a moderate oven until golden in color. Remove from heat. Serve cold.

Spinach Filling:

Ingredients:
1 kg chopped fresh spinach
3 finely chopped onions
½ a cup chopped fresh mint leaves
½ a cup chopped fresh flat parsley
3 tablespoons salt
½ a cup lemon juice
¼ cup olive oil
1 tablespoon sumac
Salt and pepper to season

Method:
1. Place all in a colander. Sprinkle quarter cup of salt. Knead well until all the juice comes out and squeeze, then place in a bowl.
2. Add half cup lemon juice to the bowl.
3. Add quarter cup olive oil, one tablespoon of sumac, salt and black pepper to season.
4. Combine well with spinach and fill the dough with the mix.

Almond Meat Samosa

Ingredients:
550g minced meat
5 cloves crushed garlic
2 finely chopped onions
2 tablespoons oil
1 ½ teaspoons small ginger
1 ¼ cup small raisins
½ a cup chopped fresh coriander
½ a cup ground almonds
250g Samoa's pastry
Sprinkle of salt
1 ½ teaspoons ground cinnamon
1 ½ teaspoons ground cumin

Method:
1. Heat the oil in pan. Cook onions and garlic until soft. Add meat breaking any lumps until browned. Stir in spices and mix well.
2. Combine raisins, almonds and coriander with meat mixture and leave aside to cool.
3. Place 2 tablespoons of the filling at the end of strip. Fold the pastry over to enclose the filling and form a triangle. Keep folding triangles until reaching end of pastry.
4. Brush triangles with oil. Place them on a baking tray, and bake until pastry is golden brown.

Dipping Sauce:

Ingredients:
2 cups plain yoghurt
1 ½ tablespoons lemon juice
1 tablespoon ground cumin
2 teaspoons sugar
Sprinkle of chili powder

Method:
Combine all ingredients in a bowl and mix well.

Lahim Bil Ajin

Dough:

Ingredients:
Similar to the recipe used for Spinach Fatair. (Ref: pg 66)

Filling Ingredients:
- 1 kg fine minced meat
- 7 cloves crushed garlic
- 2 red capsicums
- 3 onions
- 3 tomatoes
- 1 cup parsley
- 1 teaspoon salt
- ½ a teaspoon white pepper
- ¼ teaspoon cinnamon

Method:
1. Combine garlic, capsicum, onions, tomatoes, parsley and seasonings in a food processor and process until creamy. Add over meat and fold gently.
2. Flatten dough to medium circles making around 10 pieces 1cm thick. Spread meat mixture in a thin layer. Bake in hot oven about 15 minutes until crust is golden and meat is cooked. Serve hot with plain yoghurt aside.

Hint: Add extra shopped fresh chili for extra kick

Vegetable Samosa

Ingredients:
4 medium sweet potatoes boiled
2 finely chopped onions
2 small finely chopped red chilies
1 tablespoon grated fresh ginger
3 cloves crushed garlic
¼ cup finely chopped fresh coriander
250g Samoa's pastry
2 tablespoons oil
Sprinkle of ground nutmeg
Sprinkle of salt
½ a tablespoon cumin seeds

Method:
1. Cut sweet potatoes to small cubes. Heat the oil in a pan and cook onions and garlic until soft.
2. Add seeds, chilies, ginger and seasonings. Stir for 2 minutes and combine with potatoes and coriander. Leave aside to cool.
3. Place 1 tablespoon of filling at the end of each strip. Fold the pastry over to enclose the filling and form a triangle. Keep folding triangles to finish the pastry.
4. Brush triangles with the oil, place them on a baking tray and bake until pastry is golden brown, or deep fry and drain on absorbent paper.

Safeeha

Dough:

Ingredients:
½ a cup plain yoghurt
3 cups plain flour
1 teaspoon instant yeast
¼ cup oil
1 ½ cups water (maybe less)
Sprinkle of salt

Method:
Combine all in a bowl adding water gradually, mixing to firm dough. Knead until smooth. Place in a lightly oiled bowl to double in size.

Filling Ingredients:
500g minced meat
3 finely chopped onions
1 finely chopped medium tomato
2 tablespoons tahini paste
¼ cup pine nuts
1 tablespoon vinegar
3 tablespoons olive oil
Salt and black pepper to season

Method:
1. Fry pine nuts with the oil in a pan until lightly golden. Add onions and stir until soft. Stir in meat and cook while breaking lumps until browned.
2. Combine tomato, tahini, vinegar and seasonings. Mix well with meat mixture then heat for 2 minutes. Remove from heat and leave aside to cool.
3. Roll a medium thin dough, and cut into fluted circles. Place 1 teaspoon of meat mixture on the center of each circle. Pinch corners to form a square and bake in hot oven until golden. Serve hot or cold.

Dan's Dough

Ingredients:
3 cups whole meal flour
2 cups plain flour
2 cups water
¼ cup oil
1 teaspoon instant yeast
Sprinkle of sugar
Sprinkle of salt

Method:
Combine all in a bowl, mix to form a dough. Knead dough on floured surface until smooth and elastic. Place in a lightly oiled bowl to double in size.

Note: While mixing the dough, add 4 tablespoons dry thyme plus 2 chopped onions. Roll and cut with cookie cutter big size and bake until golden.

Hint: Dan's dough can be used for pizza bread

Simple Dough

Ingredients:
4 cups plain flour
1 cup oil
2 teaspoons instant yeast
1 ½ cups water
½ a teaspoon salt
½ a teaspoon sugar

Method:
Combine all in a bowl. Mix to a firm dough and knead on floured surface until smooth. Place in a bowl to double in size. Use for bread, pizza or any filling.

Lebanese Bread

Ingredients:
4 cups plain flour
2 tablespoons whole meal flour
1 ¼ cup water
1 tablespoon instant yeast
½ a teaspoon salt

Method:
1. Combine all and mix to a firm dough. Knead well until soft. Place in a lightly flour dusted bowl and cover with towel to double in size.
2. Divide dough into 16 to 18 pieces. Roll each piece on a floured surface into a 14 cm rounded bread.
3. Heat the oven well. Place bread stone inside it to heat well. Place the rounded bread on the stone and bake until lightly golden and puff.

Note: Or use an oven tray if stone is not available

Fried Dough with Meat

Ingredients:
3 cups flour
4 tablespoons ghee
4 tablespoons oil
1 cup cold water
Salt to season

Method:
1. Process flour, ghee, oil, salt and water until dough forms a ball; knead well until smooth and elastic. Cover with plastic wrap and stand for a half hour.
2. Roll dough on floured surface, cut fluted rounds on the whole pastry.
3. Place a teaspoon of filling on the center of each round, fold over to enclose filling, press edges firmly together with a fork to seal.
4. Deep fry until golden and drain on absorbent paper. Serve hot or cold.

Filling:

Ingredients:
500g minced meat
2 finely chopped onions
¼ cup pine nuts
2 tablespoons oil
Salt and black pepper to season
Cinnamon and nutmeg

Method:
Heat oil in frying pan and cook onions and pine nuts until golden. Adding the meat with the seasonings. Breaking any lumps, until these fine ingredients are cooked well. Cool aside.

Note: Freeze up to 3 months uncooked dough

Baked Dough

Dough:

Ingredients:
6 cups plain flour
6 tablespoons powdered milk
1 egg
1 cup oil
1 teaspoon baking powder
1 tablespoon lemon juice
1 tablespoon instant yeast
2 cups warm water
1 tablespoon sugar

Method:
1. Combine all in a bowl and mix to a firm dough. Knead dough until smooth. Place in a bowl and cover with towel to double in size.
2. Roll dough on a floured surface then cut fluted rounds on the dough.
3. Place half a teaspoon of mixture to the center of each round and spread it around. Place dough on an oven tray. Bake in a moderately hot oven until golden.

Filling Harhara:

Ingredients:
3 medium onions
2 red tomatoes
1 tablespoon tomato paste
½ a tablespoon chili powder
¼ teaspoon sugar
1 teaspoon ground cumin
1 teaspoon salt
1 teaspoon sumac

Method:
1. Combine all in a food processor and process for a minute.
2. Spoon the mixture in a pan. Simmer on low heat stirring occasionally to a thick sauce the leave aside to cool.
3. Spread all over the dough circles and bake in a hot oven.

Kishik:

Ingredients:
1 grated onion
½ a cup grated Kashkaval cheese
1 cup powdered kishik
2 tablespoons plain yoghurt
Olive oil
Sprinkle of chili powder
1 teaspoon toasted sesame

Method:
1. Combine all in a bowl. Add the oil gradually to form a creamy filling.
2. Roll dough to 1/8 inch thick. Using 4 cm diameter plate as a reference, cut out circles then place 1 tablespoon of filling on the center of dough circles.
3. Fold the pastry over the filling to form semi-circles and pinch the edges to form a frill and place on the tray.
4. Bake in a moderately hot oven until golden. Serve hot or cold.

Mushroom:

Ingredients:
2 finely chopped onions
300g finely chopped fresh mushrooms
1 tablespoon oyster sauce
1 tablespoon teriyaki sauce
2 tablespoons cream cheese
¼ cup grated cheddar cheese
2 tablespoons oil
Salt and pepper to season

Method:
1. Heat oil in a large frying pan and cook the onions until golden. Add mushrooms, sauces and seasonings.
2. Stir well until almost dry. Remove from heat and combine cream cheese and cheese mix well. Leave aside to cool.
3. Roll the dough lightly on a floured surface. Cut into circles using 7cm plate as reference. Place 1 teaspoon of filling on the center of the circles.
4. Fold the circles in half and press edges together firmly. Shape into semi-circles using forefingers while pressing the ends together firmly.
5. Place in an oven tray and bake in moderately heated oven until golden. Serve hot or cold.

Hashwa:

Ingredients:
500g minced meat
2 finely chopped onions
¼ cup pine nut
2 tablespoons oil
Salt and pepper to season
½ a teaspoon of ground cinnamon (Ref: pg 242)

Method:
1. Heat the oil in a frying pan. Stir pine nuts until golden. Add onions and cook until soft. Add meat and seasonings.
2. Cook until browned breaking any lumps. Remove from heat and leave aside to cool.
3. Roll dough on lightly floured surface. Cut into circles using an 8cm plate as reference. Place 1 teaspoon of filling on center of each circle.
4. Fold circles in half. Press the edges together firmly with a fork. Place in an oven tray and bake until golden. Serve hot or cold.

Za'atar:

Ingredients:
½ a cup of za'atar
Olive oil

Method:
Mix za'atar and oil in a bowl to a creamy texture and spread on circles of dough. Place on tray and bake in hot oven until golden. Serve hot.

Cheese:

Ingredients:
500g Bulgarian cheese
150g butter

Method:
Crumble cheese mix with butter. Roll dough and cut to circles. Place 1 teaspoon of filling on the center of the dough. Close to semi-circles and press edges well. Bake until golden.

Hint: Add 2 tablespoons finely chopped parsley or mint

Spring Roll Dough

Ingredients:
6 tablespoons plain flour
3 tablespoons corn flour
1 tablespoon oil
3 cups water

Method:
1. Whisk all in a medium bowl well and let stand for one hour.
2. Heat a medium size frying pan and brush it with little oil. Dip the brush in the mixture and brush inside of the pan 3 to 4 times.
3. Place over heat for a minute then remove and place on a wet towel to avoid drying.
4. Place the filling on the uncooked side. Shallow fry in a frying pan.

Filling:
30 pieces spring roll wrappers
3 carrots grated
1 small cabbage sliced thinly
4 cloves garlic finely chopped
¼ ginger root grated
2 onions grated
200g raw shrimp (small size)
1 tablespoon dry cherry
2 tablespoons soya sauce
1 tablespoon sesame oil
1 tablespoon conola oil (corn oil)

Method:
1. Heat a woke or a deep pan, add the oil.
2. Add garlic, onion and ginger, toss for a minute. Add the carrots, and cabbage, toss well to soften, stir the shrimp for a second, pour all the sauce over, toss well, remove from heat and keep aside to cool.
3. Place a spring roll on a flat dish, in a diamond shape. Put 1 tablespoon of filling above the corner, tuck the corner then the sides and roll it light.
4. Put one cup oil in a shallow pan, add the rolls from the closed part in the pan to seal. Fry until golden in color, place on a towel.

Sauce:
1 cup apple jelly or jam
½ a cup soya sauce

Method:
1. Place in a screwed jar shake well and pour in a bowl for dipping.
Or use sweet and sour sauce.

Note: can be frozen for two months.

Salty Dough

Ingredients:
227g butter at room temperature
4 cups plain flour
½ a cup oil
1 teaspoon baking powder
1 tablespoon Mahaleb powder
1 teaspoon salt

Method:
1. Combine flour, salt, baking powder and Mahaleb well. Rub in butter and oil.
2. Knead on clean surface until smooth.
3. Roll dough on floured surface until 3mm thick. Cut into many shapes using a cookie cutter.
4. Place shapes on oven trays. Brush with egg wash and sprinkle with sesame seeds or oregano or paprika. Bake in moderately heated oven until lightly browned. Cool on trays.

Salty Dough With Seasonings

Ingredients:
2 ½ cups flour
½ a teaspoon ginger
3 tablespoons sesame toasted
½ a cup ghee
¾ cup oil
Sprinkle gloves powder
2 teaspoons baking powder
1 teaspoon salt
1 teaspoon Mahalab powder

Method:
1. Combine all in a large bowl. Rub in ghee and oil. Knead well to smooth dough.
2. Roll dough on a floured surface until 2mm thick. Cut into shapes with a cookie cutter.
3. Place shapes on oven trays, brush with egg wash. Bake in a moderate oven until lightly browned. Cool on trays.

Brioche

Ingredients:
5 eggs
250g butter
1/3 cup water
4 cups plain flour
3 teaspoons instant yeast
1 teaspoon salt
¼ cup sugar

Method:
1. Combine all in a large bowl and stir until just combined. Knead on a floured surface until smooth and elastic.
2. Place dough in a large bowl, cover until doubled in size.
3. Divide dough into 8 portions and shape each portion into a sausage. Twist 2 sausages together and shape into a round or into plain sausages.
4. Place on greased oven tray and cover until the size doubles. Brush with lightly beaten egg. Sprinkle with sugar.
5. Bake in hot oven for 10 minutes then reduce heat and bake for 10 extra minutes or more until golden.

Hint: Shape to snail roll, or Twist roll, or Bow knot roll

Heidi Dough

Ingredients:
3 cups plain flour
½ a cup milk powder
¼ cup oil
1 tablespoon instant yeast
Water as required per dough
Sprinkle of salt

Method:
Combine all in a large bowl, kneading well until smooth and elastic. Cover until doubled in size.

Filling 1:
200g chopped fresh Oregano leaves
1 finely chopped medium onion
4 tablespoons lemon juice
Salt to season

Combine the whole and mix with dough, cut to rounds and bake in hot oven until lightly browned.

Filling 2:
400g Bulgarian Cheese
¼ cup chopped fresh parsley
¼ cup chopped fresh mint leaves
100g soft butter
Sprinkle of chili powder

Combine all together and roll the dough. Cut to circles. Place 1 teaspoon of filling on the center of the dough. Close to semi-circles and press the edges well. Bake until golden.

Simple Croissant

Ingredients:
2 cups milk
5 cups plain flour
¾ cup oil
2 eggs
2 tablespoons instant yeast
1 cup creamy cheese (200g)
Sprinkle of salt
¼ cup sugar

Filling Ingredients:
1. Grated cheddar cheese
2. Crushed chocolate (sprinkle top of dough with cocoa)
3. Za'atar (sprinkle with sesame seeds)
4. Or plain

Method:
1. Combine milk, oil, sugar, eggs, salt, yeast and cheese in a heavy-duty mixer and mix well.
2. Add flour gradually and knead until smooth and elastic. Place it in a large bowl and cover to double in size.
3. Roll dough on floured surface. Cut dough into triangles. At one corner place the filling and roll to opposite corner .Shape into horse shoe shape.
4. Place on a greased baking tray, cover to double in size and brush with egg wash.
5. Sprinkle the filling on top. Bake in hot oven until golden brown.

Hint: Make them small size, they will puff in the oven

Grilled Dough

Ingredients:
3 cups flour
½ a teaspoon bicarbonate of soda
½ a cup milk
1/3 cup olive oil
1/3 cup warm water
2 teaspoons salt

Method:
1. Combine all in a bowl to form a stiff sticky dough.
2. Knead dough on floured surface until smooth and elastic.
3. Leave the dough to rest for 15 minutes in a bowl.
4. Divide dough into 10 equal sized pieces. Roll the dough pieces to form a paper-thin circles.
5. Immediately place the rolled out dough on a preheated pan until lightly golden and flip to the other side.
6. Pile the dough on to one another on a wire rack. Leave to cool as the dough becomes crispy. Serve with dipping.

Onion Rings

Ingredients:
1 onion
1 cup flour
½ a teaspoon bicarbonate of soda
1 egg
2 cups water
Salt to season

Method:
1. Cut the onion into rings or circles and soak in iced water for 2 hours
2. Whisk all together to a smooth batter.
3. Dry the onion rings and dip into batter. Deep fry until golden.

Sweet Rolls

Ingredients:
3 ½ cups plain flour
2 eggs
2 tablespoons soft butter
¼ cup water
2 tablespoons honey
½ a cup milk
1 ½ teaspoons instant yeast
¼ cup sugar

Method:
1. Combine all in a heavy-duty mixer. Knead until smooth and elastic.
2. Place in a bowl and cover until doubled in size.
3. Punch down the dough. Knead and divide into 16 equal sized parts. Roll each portion to a rope shape. Coil tightly and tuck under the end to seal.
4. Place a part on greased trays, brush each with water and sprinkle sugar on top then cover with a towel until doubled in size.
5. Bake in hot oven until lightly browned for 15 to 20 minutes.

Olive Bread

Ingredients:
3 cups plain flour
1 ¼ cup warm water
1 teaspoon instant yeast
4 tablespoons olive oil
½ a teaspoon sugar
½ a teaspoon salt

Method:
1. Combine all in a large bowl. Knead well until soft and elastic. Cover to double in size.
2. Roll the dough on a floured surface to form a 24cm thick round. Place on baking sheet and cover to double in size.
3. Press some black olives onto the surface of the dough to form dimples. Brush with oil.
4. Bake in a hot oven until golden browned. Cool on a wire rack.

Saj Bread

Ingredients:
2/3 cup whole meal flour
1/3 cup plain flour
1 teaspoon of instant yeast
½ a cup water (or extra)
Sprinkle of Salt

Method:
1. Combine all in a large bowl, knead well until soft and non sticky. Cover to double in size.
2. Divide dough into 8 equal sized pieces on a floured surface. Roll out each piece to form a very thin layer.
3. Heat a large woke upside down, brush with water then place one circled shape on top, pulling the edges to form a bigger circle.
4. Remove from heat when lightly golden. Cover with towel.

Falafel

Ingredients:
2 cups dried split broad fava beans
1 cup dried chick peas
2 roughly chopped medium onions
10 garlic cloves roughly chopped
2 green chilies
1 teaspoon bicarbonate soda
1 bunch chopped fresh flat parsley
3 teaspoons ground cumin
4 teaspoons salt

Method:
1. Soak broad fava beans and chick peas in water overnight. Drain and place in a large bowl.
2. Combine onions, garlic, chilies, cumin, salt, parsley and bicarbonate of soda with the beans.
3. Place them in batches in a food processor and process until the mixture forms a rough paste.
4. Using your hands shape a tablespoon of falafel into balls and flatten slightly. Heat the oil in deep pan and cook falafel in batches until browned. Remove with a slotted spoon, drain well.
5. Serve with Lebanese bread, pickles, sliced tomatoes and tahini sauce (Ref. pg 72-48-117).

Soups

A soup is not the work of one man, it is the result of a constantly refined tradition, recipes from great grandmothers to their daughter's daughter. A soup has more power to heal a human being than any medication, it's an authentic heritage from one generation to the other.

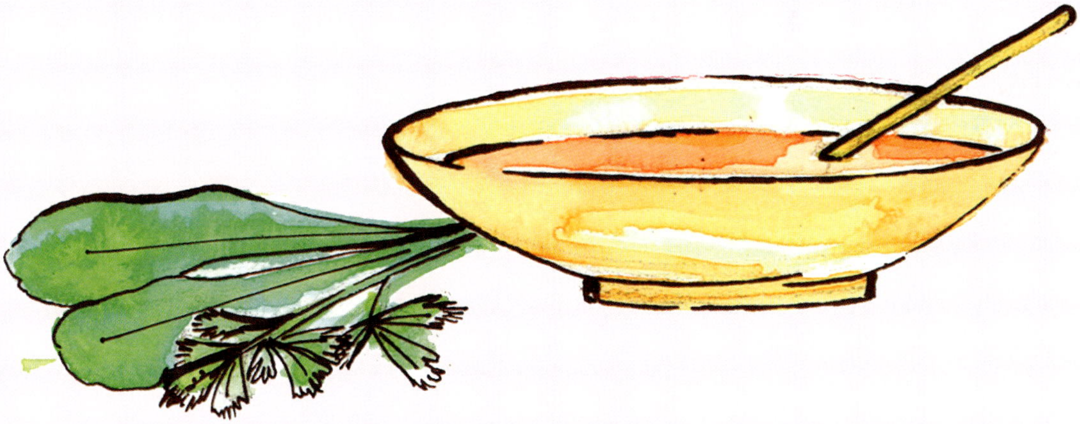

Chicken Soup with Rice

Ingredients:
1 whole chicken (cleaned)
¼ cup short grain rice
2 finely chopped onions
1 extra chopped onion
1 chopped leek
1 thinly chopped celery stick
1 chopped carrot
1 bay leaf
1 tablespoon butter
1 cinnamon stick
4 whole black peppers
½ a teaspoon grounded cinnamon
Sprinkle of Salt

Method:
1. Boil the chicken with the bay leaf and the cinnamon stick until the chicken is cooked and remove any scum from the surface.
2. Add seasonings all chopped vegetables except for the extra chopped onion. Boil until tender.
3. Pour the stock through a sieve into a bowl.
4. Heat the butter in a large pan and add the extra chopped onion to cook until tender. Add the rice and the stock. Heat until the rice is cooked.
5. Shred the chicken. Add to the stock and rice. Leave to simmer for 30 minutes.
6. Serve hot with sprinkled chopped parsley.

Note: Also add whole parts of chicken.

Spinach Soup

Ingredients:
300g spinach
500g chopped sweet potatoes
3 cloves garlic chopped
1 chopped onion
1 chopped carrot
1 tablespoon olive oil
4 cups water or stock
Sprinkle of black pepper
Sprinkle of salt

Method:
1. Heat the oil in a large pan. Add the chopped onion and garlic cloves and cook until golden in color.
2. Add all the vegetables and seasoning. Bring to boil until soft.
3. Process the spinach in batches in a food processor until finely chopped.
4. Serve with some croutons. Drizzle with fresh cream.

Papaya Soup

Ingredients:
300g chopped green papaya
100g sliced ginger
1 chopped onion
2 crushed cloves garlic
1 chopped green capsicum
1 chopped green chili pepper
1 boiled chicken (reserve stock)
1 tablespoon olive oil
Sprinkle of black pepper
Sprinkle of salt

Method:
1. Heat the oil in a large pan. Fry the onion and garlic and cook until tender.
2. Add the ginger, capsicum, chili and green papaya. Pour over the chicken stock and simmer at low heat until the vegetables are tender.
3. Add the seasonings and serve with a slice of lime.

Meat and Vegetables Soup

Ingredients:
500g beef bones boiled (reserve the stock)
1 finely chopped onion
1 cup frozen or fresh peas
1 whole tomato chopped
4 chopped zucchinis
3 chopped carrots
½ a cup vermicelli
1 tablespoon olive oil
1 bay leaf
Sprinkle of Salt
Sprinkle of pepper
1 teaspoon cinnamon powder

Method:
1. Heat the oil in a large pan. Add all chopped vegetables and cook until tender.
2. Add the beef bones, stock and simmer at low heat.
3. Add the vermicelli and seasonings. Simmer for another 5 minutes.
4. Add the meat bones and cook until boiled. Reduce the heat and simmer for another 10 minutes.
5. Serve with a slice of lemon.

Pasta Lentil Soup

Ingredients:
250g shell pasta or spiral boiled
2 cups brown lentils
500g chopped silver beet
2 finely chopped onions
5 gloves chopped garlic
3 tablespoons olive oil
½ a cup lemon juice
4 cups water
2 tablespoons plain flour
Sprinkle of salt
Sprinkle of pepper
1 teaspoon ground cumin
2 tablespoons turmeric spices

Method:
1. Place the lentils with the water in a pan and boil until tender.
2. Heat the oil in a large pan. Fry the onions and the garlic and cook until softened.
3. Add the cooked pasta with the seasonings, the boiled lentils with their water, the chopped silver beet and stir constantly for 10 minutes until tender.
4. Mix the flour with ¼ cup of water. Add to the soup while stirring until it thickens.
5. Pour the lemon juice and serve.

Milk Soup

Ingredients:
300g spiral pasta or bow
100g unsalted butter
5 cups milk
1 cup chicken stock
2 tablespoons flour
Sprinkle of white pepper
Sprinkle of nutmeg
Sprinkle of salt

Method:
1. Place the milk and the stock in a large pan and heat until boiled. Add the pasta to simmer at low heat until soft.
2. Add the butter and the seasonings. Stir frequently for 5 minutes.
3. Mix the flour with ¼ cup of water and add to the soup while stirring.
4. Serve with extra grated nutmeg.

Lentil and Potato Soup

Ingredients:
2 cups brown lentil
500g chopped potatoes
500g chopped silver beets
2 finely chopped onions
4 cups water
3 tablespoons olive oil
¼ cup lemon juice
Sprinkle of salt
Sprinkle of pepper
Sprinkle of cinnamon

Method:
1. Place the lentils with the water in a pan and boil until tender.
2. Heat the oil in a large pan. Add the onions and cook until brown in color.
3. Add the lentils and their water, potatoes and the silver beets and simmer for 30 minutes until soft.
4. Add the seasonings with the lemon juice. Simmer at low heat for 10 minutes.
5. Serve with extra lemon juice.

Special Seafood Soup

Step 1:

Ingredients:
1 kg peeled prawns
2 tablespoons oil
2 tablespoons fish sauce
3 kaffir lime leaves
200g fish ball packet
200g shrimp ball packet
200g dried rice vermicelli
300g bean sprouts
2 tablespoons brown sugar
1 cup coconut milk powder
6 cups water or fish stock

Step 2:

Ingredients:
4 chopped fresh red chilies
1 chopped onion
4 cloves chopped garlic
1 tablespoon chopped fresh ginger
2 chopped lemongrass
3 teaspoons shrimp paste
1 ½ tablespoons ground coriander
1 teaspoon ground turmeric

Method:
1. In a food processor place chilies, onion, garlic, ginger, lemon grass, shrimp paste, ground coriander and ground turmeric; process into a paste.
2. Heat oil in a large pan; add the paste and fry until fragment.
3. Add the stock or water. Boil well, strain the stock and pour into a deep pot, add coconut milk and the sugar, simmer for 10 min.
4. Add the prawns, fish sauce, lime leaves, fish and shrimp balls, sugar; simmer on low heat.
5. Soak rice vermicelli in a bowl of boiling water for 5 minutes; remove from water; add to the soup and simmer for 5 more minutes, then add bean sprouts and serve.

Carrot Soup

Ingredients:
500g chopped carrots
250g fresh cream
4 chopped onions
1 chopped potato
4 cups water or vegetable stock
2 tablespoons olive oil
Sprinkle of salt
Sprinkle of black pepper

Method:
1. Heat the oil in a large pan. Add the onions and cook for 10 minutes until soft and golden in color.
2. Add the carrots and the potato. Toss until slightly brown.
3. Pour in the stock or water and boil. Reduce the heat then simmer for 30 minutes.
4. Pour all in a food processor. Process until the mix becomes smooth and turns to a soft puree.
5. Add the seasonings and cream.
Reheat and serve.

Kishik Soup

Ingredients:
1 cup Kishik powder
2 sliced onions
4 cloves sliced garlic
5 cups water
2 tablespoons ghee

Method:
1. Heat the ghee butter in a large pan. Add the onions and garlic and cook until golden in color.
2. Add the Kishik and water. Stir constantly until boiled.
3. If the mix remains too thick, add little water and stir.
4. Serve it with Lebanese bread.

Note:
1. You may also add 250g minced meat while frying the onion.
2. Or, add with the mince meat thinly sliced cabbage.

Red Lentil Soup

Ingredients:
500g red lentils
5 cloves chopped garlic
2 chopped tomatoes
1 chopped potato
1 chopped carrot
1 chopped onion
5 cups water
One lemon juice
2 tablespoons olive oil
Sprinkle of salt
Sprinkle of pepper
Sprinkle of cumin

Method:
1. Heat oil in a large pan. Cook the onion, garlic, potato, carrot and tomatoes until soft.
2. Add the red lentils and stir frequently over 10 minutes. Add the water and boil until tender.
3. Place the soup in a food processor. Process until it becomes a soft puree.
4. Add the seasonings and lemon juice then re-heat for 5 minutes. Serve with a sprinkle of croutons on top.

Cold Soup

Ingredients:
500g red tomatoes
2 chopped Lebanese cucumbers
1 finely chopped spring onion
2 cloves crushed garlic
1 chopped yellow capsicum
1 chopped green chili (optional)
1/3 cup vinegar
¼ cup olive oil
Sprinkle of salt
Sprinkle of black pepper

Method:
1. Peel the tomato skin and chop very finely for it to reach puree form.
2. Mix the vegetables into the tomato puree. Add oil and season well.
3. Add a cup of iced water and mix well. Serve cold with the chopped spring onion.

Barley Soup

Ingredients:
1 cup barley
8 lamb shanks
2 large chopped onions
2 cloves crushed garlic
2 potatoes cut into cubes
400g sliced fresh tomatoes
5 cups beef stock
2 tablespoons olive oil

Method:
1. Heat the oil in a large pan. Place the meat and cook until brown. Remove and place in a different container.
2. Add the onions and the garlic to the pan and cook for 5 minutes.
3. Add the meat, tomatoes, potatoes and the beef stock to simmer until soft.
4. Wash the barley and add to the soup then boil.
5. Reduce the heat and simmer for 20 minutes until the barley is cooked. Serve hot.

The easy way for stock preparation

1. Vegetable Stock

Ingredients:
2 chopped onions
3 cloves chopped garlic
4 chopped carrots
2 bay leaves
2 chopped celery sticks
6 black pepper corns
6 cups water
1 tablespoon oil

Method:
1. Heat the oil in a large pan. Add the vegetables and cook for 3 minutes.
2. Add the water and boil.
3. Add the black pepper corns and simmer for 30 minutes.
4. Ladle the stock through a sieve to a bowl.

2. Fish Stock

Ingredients:
500g fish bones
200g shrimp shells
2 chopped onions
1 chopped celery
1 chopped carrot
6 cups water
5 black pepper corns

Method:
1. In a large pan place the fish bones, shrimp shells and the vegetables with the water and boil for an hour.
2. Ladle the stock through a sieve to a bowl.

3. Beef Stock

Ingredients:
1 kg beef bones
2 chopped carrots
3 chopped onions
1 bay leaf
5 cups water
5 black pepper corns

Method:
1. Place the water, the bones and the vegetables in a large pan and boil for an hour.
2. Ladle the stock through a sieve to a bowl.

4. Chicken Stock

Ingredients:
1 kg chicken bones
2 chopped carrots
2 chopped onions
5 cups water
5 black pepper corns

Method:
1. Place the water, the bones and the vegetables in large pan and boil for an hour.
2. Ladle the stock through a sieve to a bowl.

Pasta and Rice

Without rice and pasta, even the cleverest housewife cannot cook, Rice goes with all kinds of food, it's a neutral medium, like a white canvas that you can add any color to, your masterpiece to work with.

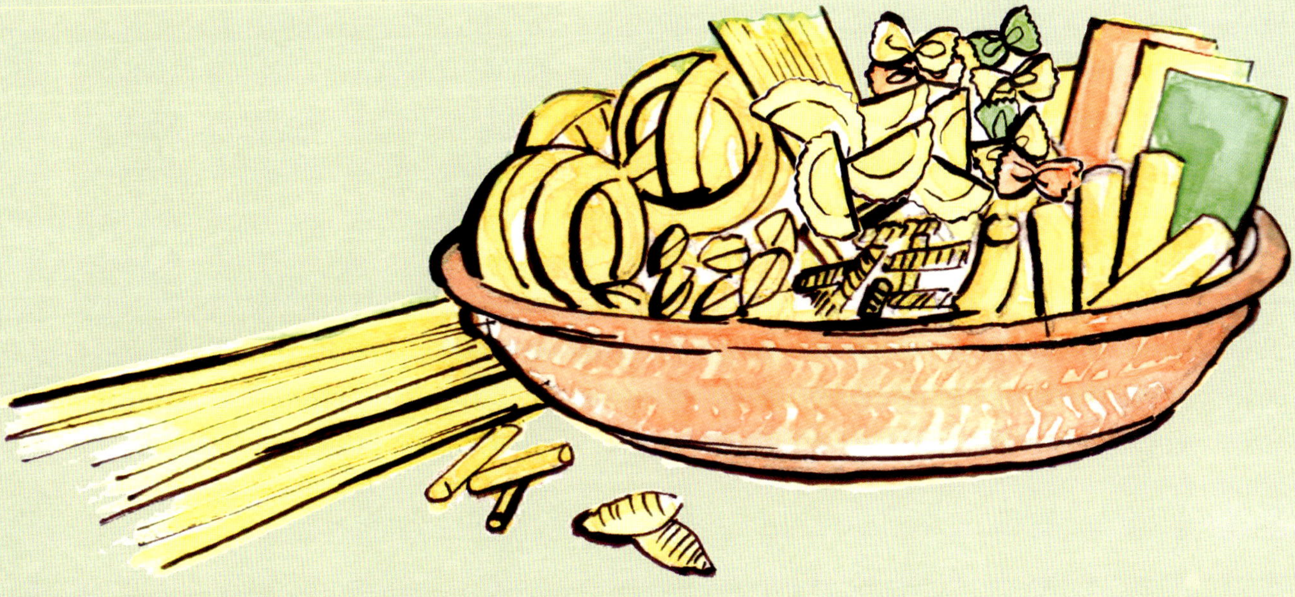

Plain Rice

Ingredients:
1 cup Basmati rice
1 ½ cups water or chicken stock
1 tablespoon ghee
1 ½ teaspoons salt

Method:
1. Heat ghee in a medium pan; stir in rice and stock. Simmer for 10 minutes until cooked.
2. Remove from heat and stand covered for 10 minutes before serving.

Herbed Rice

Ingredients:
1 cup basmati rice
1 finely chopped onion
2 cloves crushed garlic
5 finely chopped fresh mints
1 tablespoon ghee butter
1 ½ cups water or chicken stock
2 tablespoons fresh chopped coriander
1 teaspoon salt
1 teaspoon sweet paprika

Method:
1. Heat the ghee butter in a pan and cook the onion and the garlic until tender.
2. Add the rice, stock, salt, paprika, mint and coriander. Cook for 15 minutes at low heat.
3. Remove from heat.
4. Fluff the rice with a fork, and keep covered.

Rice With Vermicelli

Ingredients:
1 cup basmati rice
1 ½ cups vermicelli
1 ½ cups water or chicken stock
1 tablespoon ghee butter
1 ½ teaspoons salt

Method:
1. Heat the ghee butter in a medium pan. Add the vermicelli and cook while stirring until brown.
2. Add the stock and simmer for 2 minutes.
3. Add the rice and simmer for 10 minutes.
4. Remove from heat and keep covered for 10 minutes before serving.

Dry Rice

Ingredients:
1 cup basmati rice
1 ¾ cups water
1 tablespoon melted ghee
1 tablespoon salt

Method:
1. In a large pan stir in rice with water, salt and bring to boil until cooked.
2. Pour the rice through a sieve and keep it warm.
3. In the same pan, drizzle some of the ghee; add the rice and drizzle the rest on top; simmer on low heat for 20 minutes.
4. Remove from heat; stand covered for 10 minutes then turn over a plate to have a crunchy topping.

Rice With Chickpeas

Ingredients:
1 cup basmati rice
½ a cup chickpeas
1 finely chopped onion
1 ½ cups water
2 tablespoons olive oil
1 teaspoon salt
½ a teaspoon sweet pepper

Method:
1. Soak the chickpeas over night in a large pan.
2. Add water and boil until tender, or use canned chick peas.
3. Heat the oil in a large pan and cook the onions until golden in color.
4. Add the boiled chickpeas and the seasonings and stir well.
5. Add water and rice and stir well simmer for 15 to 20 minutes at low heat. Remove from heat and cover for 5 minutes.
6. Serve with plain yoghurt or green salad.

Machbous Cham

Ingredients:
1 kg chopped beef or lamb meat
1 teaspoon coriander seeds,
4 cinnamon sticks
4 bay leaves
1 tablespoon salt
1 teaspoon whole black pepper
1 whole nutmeg
1 teaspoon whole cardamom seeds
Sprinkle of turmeric curry powder

Method:
1. In a large pan boil the meat with all the seasonings until tender.
2. Ladle the stock through a sieve to a bowl and cover the meat to keep warm.
3. Place the stock in the pan. Add 1 tablespoon of salt, a sprinkle of turmeric curry powder and simmer for 5 minutes.
4. Stir in the rice and cook for 15 minutes at low heat.
5. Remove from heat and keep covered for 10 minutes.

Filling:
Ingredients:

7 chopped onions
200g raisins soaked in water
200g boiled yellow split peas
Sprinkle of salt
Sprinkle of black pepper
Sprinkle of ground cardamom
Sprinkle of lime powder
1 teaspoon sugar

Method:
In a deep frying pan heat the oil and cook onion until brown in color. Add the raisins, yellow split peas and seasonings. Remove from heat and maintain covered.

Sauce:

5 cloves garlic
20g fresh ginger
4 tomatoes
2 green chilies
4 tablespoons olive oil
½ a teaspoon salt
½ a teaspoon black pepper

Process all vegetables to a paste in a food processor. In a medium pan, add the seasonings to the paste while heating then simmer for 10 minutes at lower heat.

To serve:

Place the rice on a serving plate, spread the filling on top and add the lamb meat. Serve with the sauce on the side.

Rice With Tomato

Ingredients:
1 cup Basmati rice
250g fresh tomato puree
1 finely chopped onion
1 cup water or stock
4 tablespoons olive oil
1 teaspoon salt
½ a teaspoon black pepper
Sprinkle of sugar

Method:
1. Heat the oil in a pan. Add the onion and stir until tender. Add the tomato puree and the seasonings with a sprinkle of sugar. Simmer for 10 minutes.
2. Add the rice and cook for 15 minutes at low heat while stirring occasionally. Remove from heat and keep covered for 5 minutes.
3. The rice should be creamy and soft.

Note: You may add 250g of minced meat while cooking the onion.

Mouhamara (Rice)

Ingredients:
2 cups Basmati rice
3 cups chicken or fish stock
1 teaspoon salt
1 teaspoon cinnamon powder
½ a teaspoon mixed pepper
1 tablespoon sugar

Method:
In a large pan stir sugar on low heat until caramelized. Stir in the stock with the seasonings. Simmer for 5 minutes then place the rice at low heat for 15 to 20 minutes until cooked. Remove from heat and keep covered for 10 minutes.

Filling:

Ingredients:
6 sliced onions
5 cloves sliced garlic
3 finely chopped tomatoes
1 tablespoon tomato paste
3 tablespoons olive oil
1 teaspoon salt
1 teaspoon coriander powder
1 teaspoon cumin powder

Method:
In a deep frying pan, heat the oil and cook the onion until brown. Add the garlic, tomatoes and seasonings stirring frequently to a thick sauce. Remove from heat.

Fish:

Ingredients:

2 whole fish (1 kg)

Method:
1. Clean and wash the fish and keep aside. In a bowl combine lemon juice, cumin powder, crushed garlic, salt, oil.
2. Place the fish in tray, pour the filling inside out, cover with aluminum, bake in a hot oven until tender. Remove from oven.

Note: Or fry the fish without filling and place them over the rice

To Serve:

Place the rice on the plate, drizzle with some of the filling and put the fish on top and the rest of filling, place in a bowl for extra sauce.

Chicken Rice

Ingredients:
1 whole chicken cut to 6 pieces
350g minced meat
3 cups Basmati rice
¼ cup fried pine nuts
5 ½ cups water
2 tablespoons oil
1 bay leaf
2 cinnamon sticks
1 teaspoon salt
½ a teaspoon pepper
½ a teaspoon nutmeg
1 onion chopped

Method:
1. Heat the oil in a large pan and fry the onion until brown in color.
2. Add the chicken and cook until golden.
3. Add the water with all the seasonings, the bay leaf, cinnamon sticks and simmer on low heat until the chicken is tender. Remove the froth from the surface as the chicken gets cooked. Remove from heat.
4. Ladle the stock through a sieve in a large pan.
5. Cook the minced meat in a frying pan and the stock with the pine nuts. Simmer for 5 minutes.
6. Stir the rice and simmer at low heat for around 15 minutes until cooked. Remove from heat and keep covered for 10 minutes.
7. Place the rice into the plate with pieces of chicken on top.
8. Serve with green salad or yoghurt.

Paella

Ingredients:
2 chicken breast fillets cut into cubes
3 cups rice
300g calamari rings
500g raw prawns
200g oysters
150g skinless white fish fillet
2 finely chopped onions
2 finely chopped red capsicums
2 chopped tomatoes
200g fresh or frozen peas
8 cloves crushed garlic
100g finely chopped fresh parsley
1 tablespoon tomato paste
2 cups chicken stock
¼ cup olive oil
3 teaspoons salt
½ a teaspoon turmeric
¼ teaspoon saffron threads
1 teaspoon cinnamon powder
Sprinkle of Cayenne pepper

Method:
1. Peel the prawns and remove the dark veins.
2. Scrub oysters and clean to remove the hairy beards. Place in a pan with water, and boil for 2 to 3 minutes. The shell should open up when the oyster is cooked. Remove the oysters that remain closed. Reserve the liquid.
3. Heat the oil in a large frying pan and cook the chicken until golden brown in color. Remove from the pan and set aside. Add the prawns, calamari, fish and cook for 1 to 2 minutes. Remove from the pan and set aside.
4. Heat extra oil in the pan. Add the onions, garlic, tomatoes and red capsicum to cook for 5 minutes until the onion is soft. Add the tomato paste, the reserved liquid and seasonings. Add the rice with the saffron and mix well.
5. Bring slowly to boil. Reduce heat and simmer uncovered for 15 to 20 minutes.
6. Place the peas, chicken, prawns, calamari, fish and stock. Cover and cook at low heat for 10 to 15 minutes. Stir until the rice is tender and the sea food is cooked.
7. Add the oysters on top and cook for one more minute. Serve with sprinkled parsley.

Rice with Fish (Saiadiat sammak)

Ingredients:
4 fried fish fillets
2 fish bones
3 cups of basmati rice or long grain rice
1 bay leaf
1 chopped carrot
1 chopped onion
2 tablespoons dry lime powder
1 teaspoon ginger powder
1 teaspoon cumin powder
½ a teaspoon cinnamon powder
1 teaspoon salt
½ a teaspoon white pepper

Method:
Heat 1 tablespoon of oil in a large pan and fry the onion until golden brown. Add the remaining ingredients with 4 to 5 cups of water and boil over high heat for 10 minutes then simmer at low heat for 10 minutes. Remove from heat and ladle the stock into a sieve over the bowl. Use the stock to cook the rice. Serve the cooked fish on top of the rice.

Spicy Sauce:

Ingredients:
2 finely chopped onions
5 cloves crushed garlic
2 finely chopped red chilies
1 sliced green capsicum
3 finely chopped tomatoes
5 tablespoons chopped fresh coriander
¼ cup olive oil

Method:
Heat the oil in a medium pan and fry the onions and garlic until golden. Add the capsicum, chilies, salt, pepper, tomatoes and coriander. Stir well while simmering at low heat for 5 minutes. Add ¼ cup of fish stock to boil for 3 minutes. Remove from heat and serve with the rice or any baked, grilled or fried fish.

Tahini Sauce:

Ingredients:
2 small finely chopped onions
3 cloves crushed garlic
1 finely chopped red capsicum
4 tablespoons of finely chopped fresh coriander
3 tablespoons ground almond
4 tablespoons tahini
½ a cup lemon juice
½ a cup water

Method:
Heat oil in a medium pan and fry the onions and garlic until soft. Add capsicum, almond, and coriander. Stir well. Add water, lemon juice, tahini, salt and pepper to boil, while stirring to a medium thick sauce. Serve hot or cold with the rice and grilled or fried fish.

Vegetable Biriyani

Ingredients:
2 cups basmati rice
4 cups water
1 cinnamon stick
¼ teaspoon saffron threads
6 whole black peppers

Method:
Bring water to boil in a medium pan with the saffron. Stir in the rice, and simmer until cooked. Remove from heat and keep covered.

Vegetables Ingredients:

Ingredients:
2 green chilies cut in length
2 carrots sliced to thin sticks
1 small cauliflower
2 potatoes cut to small cubes
1 chopped onion
4 crushed garlic cloves
5 chopped curry leaves
2 tablespoons of chopped coriander
½ a cup chicken or vegetables stock
¼ cup oil
1 teaspoon salt
2 teaspoons turmeric powder
1 teaspoon curry powder
1 teaspoon coriander powder
1 teaspoon black pepper

Method:
1. Heat oil in a large pan. Cook the onion, garlic and curry leaves until the onion is brown in color.
2. Add all the seasonings and stir until the fragrance gets stronger. Add all the remaining vegetables with the stock and simmer until soft. Remove from heat and place all in a bowl.
3. In the same pan, place half of the rice at the bottom, place the vegetables on the rice and cover with rest of the rice.
4. Simmer at low heat for 15 minutes. Remove from heat and maintain in the pan for 5 additional minutes.
5. Turn over a big plate to serve.

Rice With Lentil (Midardarah)

Ingredients:
1 cup brown lentils
½ a cup basmati rice or short grain rice
4 sliced onions
1 finely chopped onion
3 cups water
¼ cup olive oil
Sprinkle of salt
½ a teaspoon cumin

Method:
1. Put the lentils in a pan. Cover with water and boil until half cooked. Add the seasonings and cook for 5 minutes.
2. Cook the finely chopped onion until golden in color and add over lentil.
3. Stir in the rice and simmer at low heat until cooked. Use a fork to fluff then remove from heat and keep covered for 10 minutes.
4. Heat the oil in a frying pan and cook the sliced onions until brown and crisp. Remove from oil and keep aside.
5. Use a fork to fluff lentil. Serve on a plate with crispy onions sprinkled over the rice.
Serve with plain yoghurt or cabbage salad.
(Ref. pg 262-28)

Shrimp Biriyani

Ingredients:
Mix 500g raw prawns with the following and leave to soak for 30 minutes:
- ½ a cup lemon juice
- ½ a teaspoon turmeric
- ½ a teaspoon black pepper
- ½ a teaspoon coriander powder
- ½ a teaspoon cinnamon powder
- ½ a teaspoon cardamom powder

2 cups basmati rice boiled and drained
2 chopped onions
5 chopped garlic cloves
1 tablespoon fresh grated ginger
3 sliced green chilies (optional)
1 large potato cut to small cubes and fried
4 cups fish stock or water
4 tablespoons olive oil
2 tablespoons chopped coriander

Method:
1. Heat the oil in a large pan. Cook the onion and the garlic until brown in color.
2. Add the shrimps and keep stirring until their color changes.
3. Stir in the chilies, ginger, potato and coriander. Simmer at low heat for 5 minutes then remove from heat and place in a bowl.
4. Add water or stock to the pan, stir the rice and boil for 8 minutes then simmer until the rice is tender.
5. Place a layer of rice in the bottom of the pan, topped with shrimps' filling and cover with the rest of the rice. Drizzle little ghee butter on top.
6. Cook at low heat for 10 minutes. Turn over a plate and serve.

Rice With Lentil (Masafaieh)

Ingredients:
1 cup brown lentils
1/3 cup Basmati rice
4 thinly sliced onions
3 cups water
¼ cup olive oil
1 teaspoon salt
½ a teaspoon sweet pepper

Method:
1. Heat the oil in a pan and stir in the onions until brown and crispy. Remove from heat and place on a plate.
2. In the same pan stir in the lentils with the seasonings and water. Boil on medium heat until tender.
3. Place the lentil mix in a food processor until creamy and soft. Return to the pan.
4. Stir in the rice in the lentil sauce. Simmer at low heat stirring occasionally until the rice is cooked and creamy.
5. Serve in a plate with sprinkled onions and drizzle with extra olive oil.

Chicken Biriyani

Ingredients:
1 whole chicken chopped
2 cups Basmati rice
2 chopped onions
4 chopped garlic cloves
1 teaspoon fresh diced ginger
2 green or red sliced chilies
2 chopped tomatoes
1 cup yoghurt
2 ½ cups water
2 tablespoons ghee butter
½ a teaspoon salt
½ a teaspoon turmeric
½ a teaspoon black pepper
½ a teaspoon turmeric powder
½ a teaspoon coriander powder
½ a teaspoon cardamom powder
½ a teaspoon cinnamon powder

Method:
1. Combine chicken, chilies, coriander, cardamom, black pepper, turmeric, salt and yoghurt in a medium bowl. Cover and refrigerate for 1 hour.
2. Heat the ghee butter in a large pan. Add the onions, garlic, ginger and tomatoes and stir until tender.
3. Add the chicken mixture and simmer covered while stirring occasionally until the chicken is tender. Remove froth from surface and reserve the stock.
4. Stir in the rice and the stock into the chicken mixture. Boil then simmer covered about 15 minutes. Stir occasionally until the rice is cooked.
5. OR brush the pan with a small quantity of ghee butter and spread a layer of rice topped with chicken mixture and a layer of rice drizzled with ghee to simmer at low heat for 10 to 15 minutes. Flip the pan on a plate and serve.

Note: Boil eggs, add over the chicken sauce (optional)

Meat Biriyani

Use 1kg of chopped beef steak and follow the same procedure.

Rolled Cabbage With Rice (Malfouf Mehshi)

Ingredients:
800g minced meat
500g cabbage leaves
10 peeled garlic cloves
2 cups short grain rice
3 ½ cups water or chicken stock
2 tablespoons lemon juice
3 tablespoons ghee butter
1 ½ teaspoons salt
½ a teaspoon black pepper
1 teaspoon cinnamon
1 teaspoon sweet pepper (all spice)
1 teaspoon dry mint powder

Method:
1. Bring water to boil in a large pan. Stir in the cabbage leaves until tender then place in a colander and rinse thoroughly under cold water.
2. Remove the thick stems and cut leaves to 2 or 3 pieces.
3. Mix the rice with all seasonings, minced meat and ghee butter.
4. Layout a cabbage leaf on a plate, place 2 to 3 teaspoons of filling on one end of the leaf and then roll it upwards to the other end.
5. Use the thick stems to line the base of a large pan and place the cabbage rolls on it. Add the garlic between each layer. Sprinkle dry mint. Put a plate on top of the rolls to keep them in place and cover with 3 ½ cups of water or stock and lemon juice bringing to boil. Reduce heat and simmer covered for 50 minutes. Remove the plate, serve the cabbage rolls with a spoon. Serve with plain yoghurt aside.

Rice And Peas

Ingredients:
2 cups Basmati rice
½ to 1 cup fresh or frozen peas
3 ½ cups water or stock
3 tablespoons ghee butter or olive oil
½ a teaspoon salt
½ a teaspoon cinnamon powder
½ a teaspoon cumin seeds
2 cardamom pods

Method:
1. Heat the ghee butter or the olive oil in a large pan. Add the cardamom and cumin seeds then stir for 1 minute. Stir in the cinnamon and salt.
2. Stir in the peas, stock, and rice. Bring to boil and reduce heat. Cover to simmer for 15 minutes until the rice is cooked.

Zucchini and Eggplant Stuffed with Rice (Maahashi)

Ingredients:
1kg small size zucchinis
1kg small size eggplants
1kg minced meat
4 cups short grain rice
4 tablespoons tomato paste
Chicken stock or water
3 tablespoons ghee butter
1 ½ teaspoons salt
½ a teaspoon black pepper
1 teaspoon cinnamon powder
1 teaspoon sweet pepper (also known as all spice)

Method:
1. Use a zucchini corer to hollow the zucchinis and eggplants.
2. In a large bowl combine meat, rice, ghee and seasonings and mix to blend all the ingredients perfectly. (Do not over mix)
3. In a large pan, place the tomato paste, stock and an extra sprinkle of salt.
4. Fill the zucchini and eggplants with the rice mixture. Place in the pan, cover with water and boil. Reduce the heat, simmer until cooked and sauce thickens.

Note:
1. Cook the zucchinis with grape leaves, by lining the pan with boiled lamb chops topped with grape leaves then zucchini. Only add water to cook, and cover the whole with a plate to prevent from moving.

2. Cook the zucchinis with yoghurt: Boil the zucchinis with water for 10 minutes. Place 5 cups of plain yoggurt in a pan and mix 1 tablespoon of corn flour with 3 cups of water. Add the mix to the yoggurt. Cook at low heat stirring frequently until it starts to boil. Add zucchini and cook at low heat until soft. Add a sprinkle of dry mint.

The zucchini can be cooked with yoghurt.

RICE & PASTA

Vegetarian Grape Leaves

Ingredients:
500g fresh grape leaves
2 ½ cups short grain rice
3 finely chopped onions
5 finely chopped fresh tomatoes
1 cup finely chopped parsley
1/3 cup chopped fresh mint leaves
2 tablespoons tomato paste
1 teaspoon chili paste
½ a cup olive oil
Lemon juice
1 ½ teaspoons salt
½ a teaspoon black pepper
½ a teaspoon cinnamon powder

Method:
1. Line the base of a large pan with sliced tomatoes and onions.
2. Rinse the leaves in cold water. Soak in boiling water for 1 hour and drain.
3. Heat the oil in a pan. Add the onions and cook for 5 minutes. Stir in the rice and cook for extra minutes. Remove from heat.
4. Stir in all the seasonings, tomato and chili pastes then leave to cool.
5. Add the tomatoes, parsley and mint. Mix well with lemon juice and extra olive oil.
6. Lay out a grape leaf with the grape vein side up on a plate. Place 2 teaspoons of filling, fold the sides over and roll up towards the tip of the leaf.
7. Place the leaves in the lined pan in layers. Place a plate on top to prevent from moving and cover with 1 ½ cups of water. Cook at low heat and simmer covered for 30 minutes. Remove from heat and leave to cool. Flip the pan on a plate before serving.

Grape Leaves and Meat

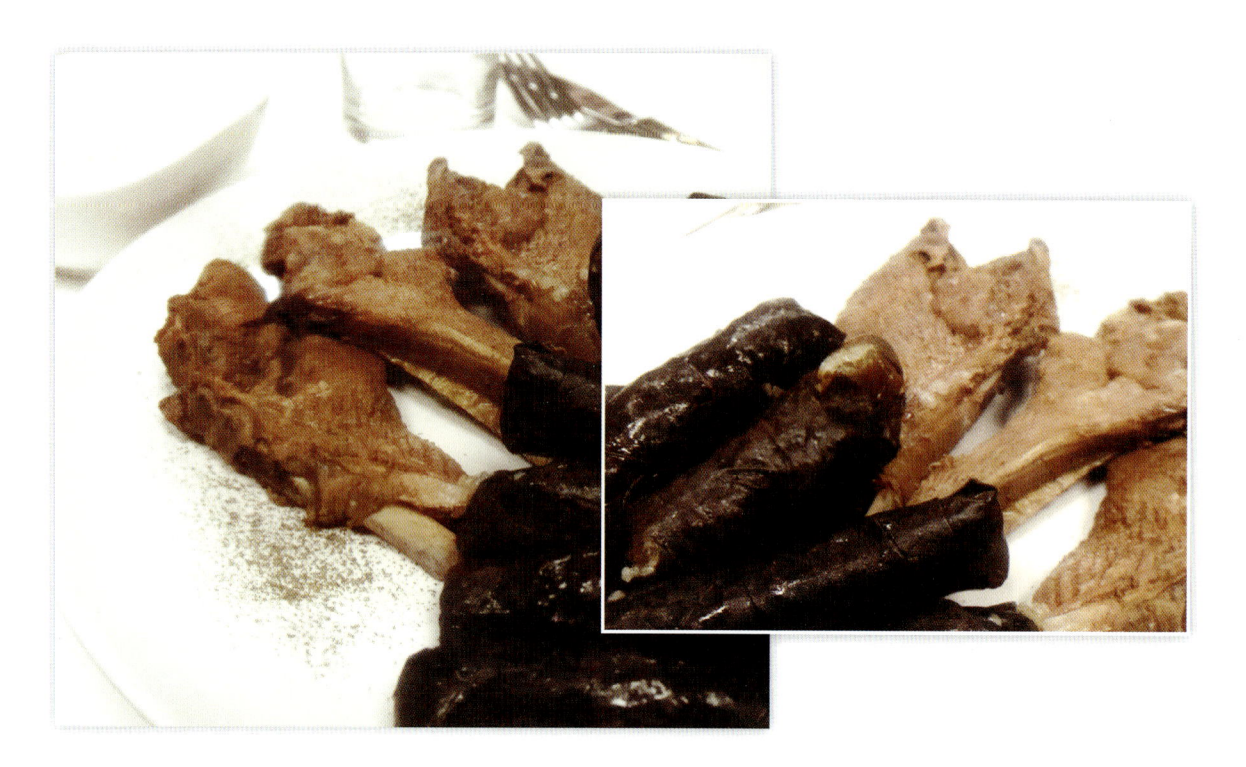

Ingredients:
500g fresh grape leaves
500g minced meat
6 pieces boiled lamb chops
1 ½ cups short grain rice
3 tablespoons ghee butter
1 ½ teaspoons salt
½ a teaspoon black pepper
½ a teaspoon cinnamon powder

Method:
1. Bring water to boil with the lamb chops for 10 minutes. Ladle the boiled lamb chops and water into a sieve. Line them in a large pan.
2. Rinse leaves in cold water. Soak in boiling water for 1 hour then drain.
3. In a big bowl stir in the rice, seasonings and ghee butter to mix well.
4. Lay out a grape leaf, with the leaf vein side up on a plate. Place 1 teaspoon of filling and fold the sides over mixture then roll up towards the tip of the leaf.
5. Place leaves in the lined pan in layers. Put a plate on top to prevent from moving and cover with 2 ½ cups of water. Bring to boil then reduce heat and simmer covered for 45 minutes. Remove from heat and lift out the leaves with a slotted spoon. Serve with yoghurt aside.

Rice Patties

Ingredients:
1 ½ cups short grain rice
1 potato
1 egg
1 teaspoon of salt
½ a teaspoon of black pepper

Filling:

Ingredients:
50g minced meat
4 finely chopped onions
¼ cup fried pine nuts
4 tablespoons olive oil
1 teaspoon salt
½ a teaspoon black pepper

Method:
1. Boil the potato and rice until tender. Drain and place back in a pan. Stir over heat and mash well. Remove from heat and leave to cool.
2. Add the seasonings and the egg. Mix well bringing to the form of dough.

Method:
1. Heat the oil in a medium pan, cook onion and pine nuts until soft. Add the minced meat and seasonings and maintain until cooked.
2. Remove from heat and leave the meat mixture to cool.
3. Place 1 tablespoon of rice mixture in one floured hand. Add 1 tablespoon of filling covered with 1 tablespoon of rice mixture and pat to the form of a ball.
4. Roll balls in flour then deep fry them in a large sauce pan of hot oil until golden brown in color. Drain on absorbent paper.

Beans Moujadara

Ingredients:
3 cups beans (any kind)
3 sliced onions
1 ½ cups cracked wheat (burghul) or short grain rice
¼ cup olive oil
1 teaspoon salt
½ a teaspoon black pepper
½ a teaspoon cinnamon powder

Method:
1. Place the beans in a large bowl and cover with water. Soak overnight, drain and rinse.
2. Heat the oil in large pan and stir in the onions until brown in color. Remove ½ the onions and drain on absorbent paper.
3. In the same pan stir in the beans, water and seasonings. Bring to boil, reduce heat and simmer uncovered for 40 minutes or until beans are tender.
4. Stir in the rice and cover to simmer for 5 minutes stirring occasionally until the rice is tender and creamy. Place the rice mixture in a plate and sprinkle the crispy onion. Serve with yoghurt or green salad aside.

Baked Pasta

Ingredients:
450g spaghetti
250g minced meat
Parmesan cheese
3 onions finely chopped
2 garlic cloves crushed
½ a cup tomato paste
2 tablespoons olive oil
1 ½ teaspoon salt
½ a teaspoon black pepper

Method:
1. Heat oil in a medium pan. Cook onion until soft, add minced meat until brown in color. Mash the meat with a spoon while cooking.
2. Add tomato paste, seasonings and 2 cups of water. Simmer at low heat until sauce is thick.
3. Cook pasta in a large pan of boiling water until tender. Drain and place in a baking tray. Pour minced meat sauce over and bake 10 to 15 minutes in an oven at moderate heat.
4. Sprinkle cheese on top and serve.

Tagliatelle Rishta

Ingredients:
500g Tagliatelle pasta
1 tablespoon flour
3 cups chicken stock
1 ¼ cup milk
4 tablespoons butter
1 tablespoon butter extra
1 ½ teaspoon salt
½ a teaspoon white pepper
Sprinkle of nutmeg

Method:
1. Add pasta to a pan of boiling chicken stock and cook until tender. Drain in a colander and place back in the pan. Set aside.
2. Melt butter in a saucepan, add flour and stir over low heat. Remove from heat and gradually add milk stirring until smooth. Return to heat, cook stirring constantly with the seasonings until the sauce boils and thickens.
3. Add sauce over pasta and mix well. Add the extra butter, sprinkle the nutmeg and stir for 1 minute. Serve hot and creamy.

Note: Mix flour and water to a firm dough, leave to rest, roll on a floured surface, cut into medium strips.
Follow the above instruction, it will be rich in flavour and creamy.

Tagliatelle with Bacon and Mushroom

Ingredients:
500g Tagliatelle pasta
200g bacon - turkey - chicken
300g fresh mushroom sliced
2 onions chopped finely
1 ¼ cups cream
2 egg yolks
50g grated Parmesan cheese
50g grated Gruyere cheese
¼ cup olive oil
1 teaspoon salt
½ a teaspoon black pepper
1 teaspoon ground nutmeg

Method:
1. Place pasta in a large pan of boiling water and cook until tender. Drain in a colander and place back in the pan. Set aside.
2. Slice the bacon and fry in a pan until crispy. Remove and drain on absorbent paper.
3. In the same pan, fry the mushroom until tender.
4. In a bowl, whisk cream, egg yolk, salt, pepper, nutmeg and Parmesan cheese well.
5. Add bacon and mushroom then pour the mixture over the pasta and toss well. Place the whole back in the pan and cook over very low heat until the mixture gets thick.
6. Place the whole in a baking tray and sprinkle Gruyere cheese. Bake at moderate heat until golden.

Note: All bacon must be smoked.

Shells with Tuna

Ingredients:
500g small shell pasta
1 tuna can
2 small onions chopped finely
7 sundried tomatoes chopped
¼ cup raisins
¼ cup pine nut
2 tablespoons fresh parsley chopped
½ a cup water
3 tablespoons olive oil
1 teaspoon salt
½ a teaspoon black pepper
½ a teaspoon dry basil or fresh leaves chopped

Method:
1. Heat oil in a medium pan. Fry pine nuts until golden. Add the onions and cook until soft.
2. Add the tuna, raisins, tomatoes, seasonings and dry basil powder while mixing well. Pour water and boil for a minute then remove from heat.
3. Add shell pasta to a large pan of boiling water and cook until tender. Drain and return to pan.
4. Add sauce and toss to mix, stir in parsley and let stand for 10 minutes before serving.

Spaghetti Tango

Ingredients:
700g minced meat
500g spaghetti
3 onions finely chopped
5 garlic cloves chopped
2 tomatoes chopped
100g coriander chopped
1 fresh chili chopped
10 fresh curry leaves chopped
½ a cup green olives deseeded and chopped
4 tablespoons tomato paste
1 ½ cups chicken stock
½ a cup olive oil
½ a teaspoon salt
½ a teaspoon black pepper
1 teaspoon mixed pepper
½ a teaspoon grounded curry powder

Note: Sauce must be thick

Method:
1. Heat oil in a medium pan. Add garlic and stir for 10 seconds. Add the onions and cook until soft. Add meat and break any lumps while cooking.
2. In the same pan, add tomatoes, coriander, chili, curry, olives and stock. Bring to boil until the sauce thickens. Add seasonings, curry powder and tomato paste and simmer at low heat for 5 minutes. Remove from heat and set aside.
3. Add spaghetti to a large pan of boiling water and cook until tender. Drain well.
4. Serve spaghetti with meat sauce on the top.

Spaghetti With Zucchini

Ingredients:
500g spaghetti or fettuccine
3 garlic cloves grated
1 medium onion grated
½ a red capsicum grated
500g zucchini grated
3 medium tomatoes
1 tablespoon fresh parsley
½ a cup olive oil
1 teaspoon salt
½ a teaspoon black pepper

Method:
1. Cook the pasta in a large pan with boiling water until tender. Drain and place back in to pan.
2. Heat the oil in a deep pan. Add onion and garlic and cook for 1 minute. Add capsicum and zucchini and cook. Stir until soft.
3. In a food processor add tomatoes, parsley and seasonings. Process well.
4. Add the sauce to the zucchini and boil for 2 minutes.
5. Add the sauce to the pasta and toss well to combine well.

Spaghetti With Yoghurt

Ingredients:
300g spaghetti
3 cups plain yoghurt
3 garlic cloves crushed
1 teaspoon salt
1 teaspoon dry mint powder

Method:
1. In a large serving bowl whisk yoghurt, garlic and salt. Mix well.
2. Cook pasta in a large pan with boiling water until tender. Drain and place under running water to cool.
3. Add pasta to yoghurt and toss well. Let stand for 10 minutes before serving. Sprinkle mint on top.

Linguine Meatball

Ingredients:
500g linguine
500g minced meat
1 egg
1 cup fresh breadcrumbs
3 tablespoons pine nut
2 tablespoons raisins
½ a cup grated Parmesan cheese
1 tablespoon chopped fresh basil
1 teaspoon salt
½ a teaspoon black pepper

Sauce:

Ingredients:
1 medium onion sliced
400g canned tomato puree
½ a cup cream
½ a cup red wine

Method:
1. In a large bowl, combine meat, egg, breadcrumbs, pine nut, raisins, cheese, basil and seasonings. Roll tablespoon full of mixture forming a ball and let aside.
2. In a pan add a tablespoon of olive oil and fry the onion until soft. In the same pan, add the tomato puree, cream, and wine. Season to taste and bring to boil.
3. Reduce heat and place the meatball in the pan. Simmer until the meat is cooked and the sauce thickens. Remove from heat.
4. Add linguine to a large pan of boiling water and cook until tender. Drain well. Serve linguine with meatball and sauce over the top.

Spaghetti Tahini

Ingredients:
500g spaghetti
½ a cup tahini (sesame paste)
1 clove crushed garlic
2 tablespoons fresh parsley chopped
1 ½ cups water
¼ cup lemon juice
1 teaspoon salt

Method:
1. Cook spaghetti in a large pan of boiling water until tender. Drain and place under running water to cool.
2. In a bowl, whisk tahini, garlic, lemon juice, salt and water to a thin paste.
3. Add spaghetti over sauce, toss well, let stand for 5 minutes. Sprinkle parsley on top and serve.

Spaghetti Garlic

Ingredients:
400g Spaghetti
6 cloves crushed garlic
¼ cup lemon juice
1/3 cup olive oil
1 teaspoon salt

Method:
1. In a large serving bowl whisk garlic, lemon juice, olive oil and salt well.
2. Cook pasta in large pan of boiling water until tender, drain well. Combine with sauce and let stand for 5 minutes before serving.

Lasagna

Ingredients:
400g packet instant lasagna sheets
1 cup grated mozzarella cheese

Method:
1. Brush an oven dish with oil. Line the lasagna sheets leaving no gaps in between.
2. Spoon ½ of the meat sauce over the lasagna sheets. Place another layer of lasagna sheets on top and spoon ½ of the cheese sauce.
3. Continue layering and finishing with cheese sauce. Sprinkle with Parmesan and bake for 40 minutes until bubbling and golden.

Meat Sauce:

Ingredients:
500g mince meat
1 medium onion finely chopped
2 garlic cloves crushed
4 tablespoons tomato paste
¾ cups water
2 tablespoons olive oil
1 ½ teaspoons salt
½ a teaspoon black pepper

Method:
1. Heat the oil in a large pan. Add onion and garlic and cook until soft. Add the meat, cook until brown, breaking any lumps while cooking.
2. Stir in the tomato paste, water and seasonings. Bring to boil. Reduce heat and simmer for 15 minutes.

Cheese Sauce:

Ingredients:
3 cups milk
½ a cup mozzarella cheese
70g butter
1/3 cup plain flour
1 teaspoon salt
1 teaspoon grated nutmeg

Method:
1. Melt the butter in the saucepan. Add flour and stir for a minute then remove from heat. Gradually add the milk while stirring until the mixture is smooth.
2. Return over low heat and cook while stirring until the sauce boils. Add salt and nutmeg, reduce heat and simmer until the sauce thickens. Remove from heat. Add cheese and mix well.

Easy Spaghetti

Ingredients:
400g spaghetti
60g butter
2 egg yolks
½ a teaspoon salt
1 cup Parmesan grated

Method:
1. Cook spaghetti in a pan of boiling water, until soft. Drain well
2. Add butter, salt and egg yolks, whisk fast until all combined. Serve with parmesan cheese on top

Spaghetti Chili

Ingredients:
500g spaghetti
1/3 cup olive oil
2 fresh chilies chopped
2 garlic cloves crushed
½ a teaspoon salt

Method:
1. Heat the oil in a medium pan. Cook garlic and chili then remove from heat.
2. Cook spaghetti in a pan of boiling water until soft. Drain well.
3. Combine pasta with chili and salt, toss well and serve.

Note: Add rocket leaf in step 3.

Tagliatelle Tomato

Ingredients:
400g Tagliatelle
2 tablespoons chopped fresh basil
400g canned crushed tomatoes
4 tablespoons olive oil
1 ½ teaspoons salt
½ a teaspoon black pepper

Method:
1. Heat the oil in a medium pan. Add tomatoes and seasonings. Bring to boil at low heat for 20 to 25 minutes. Stir in basil and remove from heat.
2. Cook pasta in a large pan of boiling water until tender, drain well and combine with sauce.

Fettuccine Sausage

Ingredients:
500g Fettuccine
5 medium sausages (any kind)
2 sliced onions
¼ cup ketchup sauce or 3 tablespoons tomato paste
300g cream
1 tablespoon butter
1 teaspoon salt
½ a teaspoon pepper

Method:
1. Heat butter in a medium pan and cook onion until soft. Add sliced sausage and stir until lightly browned.
2. Add cream, ketchup and seasonings. Stir while heating without boiling then remove from heat.
3. Cook pasta in a large pan of boiling water until tender, drain well and combine with sauce. Let stand 5min before serving.

Fettuccine Albaha

Ingredients:
500g Fettuccine
1 ½ cups cream
¼ cup chopped fresh basil
60g butter
1 cup grated Parmesan cheese (or cheddar)
1 teaspoon salt
½ a teaspoon black pepper

Method:
1. Cook pasta in a large pan of boiling water until tender, drain using a colander and replace in pan.
2. Heat the butter in a pan at low heat. Add cream, cheese, salt and pepper. Bring to boil stirring regularly.
3. Add the basil, stir the sauce over the pasta and toss well. Sprinkle extra cheese on top.

Tanourine Maakroun

Ingredients:
2 cups plain flour
1 tablespoon olive oil
¼ - ½ cup water
1 teaspoon salt

Method:
1. Place all the ingredients in a large bowl and mix using your hands to end up with firm dough.
2. Divide the dough into 5 portions; Roll each piece into a thin rope. Cut the ropes into 1cm pieces.
3. Put the pieces of dough on the rough side of a colander and press down with your finger, rolling the dough as you do so. Place on a tray lightly dusted with flour.
4. Cook Maakroun in a large pan of boiling water, until they rise to the surface. Boil for another 5 minutes then remove from water and keep aside.

Note: Can be used with any sauce.

Some sauces to mix with:

1. Kishik: Follow the same steps mentioned in kishik soup recipe. While it is boiling, add the Maakroun to cook for 10 minutes and serve.
(Ref. pg 101)

2. Garlic Dip: Take some of the boiling water of Maakroun and mix with garlic and 2 tablespoons of lemon juice. Sprinkle the salt, stir in Maakroun and serve.
(Ref. pg 18)

3. Awarma: Fry the sliced onion with Awarma until golden. Add Maakroun, toss well and serve.
(Ref. pg 253)

Tagliatelle Cheese

Ingredients:
500g Tagliatelle
400g boiled chicken (shredded)
4 cups milk
1 bay leaf
1 cinnamon stick
70g butter
3 tablespoons plain flour
2 cups grated cheddar cheese
½ a cup breadcrumbs

Method:
1. Boil tagliatelle in the same pan of chicken stock and cook until tender, drain well and return to pan keep warm.
2. In a medium pan, put milk, bay leaf and cinnamon stick bring to the boil, remove from heat, and allow standing for 30min strain into a jug.
3. Melt butter in a sauce pan, add flour and stir for 2min, remove from heat, gradually add milk mixture stirring until smooth, return to heat, stirring constantly until sauce boils and thickens, seasons with salt and pepper.
4. Spoon ½ of tagliatelle into a deep casserole dish, add sauce over it, place the chicken over the sauce, sprinkle the cheese.
5. Place the second layer of pasta, add rest of sauce over and toss well, sprinkle cheese on top of sauce and last sprinkle breadcrumbs to cover the top.
6. Bake for 20-30min until golden and serve.

Dandi

Ingredients:
500g Arisha (Ref. pg 264)
½ a cup grated Parmesan
¼ cup flour
2 egg yolks
½ a teaspoon salt
Sprinkle black pepper
Sprinkle grated nutmeg

Method:
1. In a large bowl, whisk egg yolks, seasonings and Parmesan cheese to combine well.
2. Add Arisha with flour and mix with your hands to end up with loose dough forms. Place on a lightly floured surface and knead gently. Add some flour if the dough is too sticky.
3. Roll a heaped teaspoon full of dough into oval shapes. Indent one side using the back of a fork. Cook in batches in a large pan of boiling water until it floats.
Drain well and keep warm.

Sauce:

Ingredients:
1 bunch parsley
¼ cup walnuts
4 garlic cloves
½ a cup grated Parmesan
¼ cup olive oil
Sprinkle of salt

Method:
1. Place all in a food processor. Process well until the sauce thickens and becomes creamy. Extra olive oil may be needed.
2. In a large serving plate place the dandi with the sauce on top. Sprinkle the grated Parmesan on top.

Vegetarian

A pure soul, from a pure belly, it is one of the hardest things in life to commit to that, but one of the most rewarding things as well. As they make your spirits lift high and your body age less.

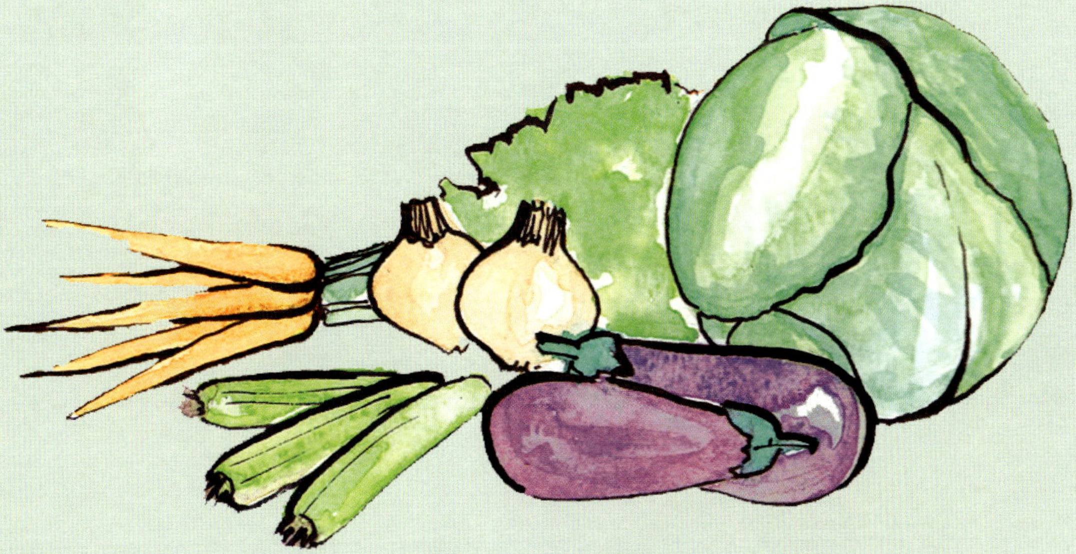

Fried EggPlant

Ingredients:
2 large or 500g eggplants thinly sliced
Oil for frying
Plain flour for dusting
Sprinkle of salt

Method:
1. Slice the eggplants and soak them in water for 15 minutes. Pat-dry in a towel then dust with flour mixed with salt.
2. Deep fry the eggplant slices a few at a time until golden then drain on absorbent paper. Serve with Lebanese bread.

Note:
1. Deep fry sliced zucchini until golden, no need to soak or dust with flour.
2. Cut cauliflower to small floret and deep fry until golden. Serve with tahini sauce. (Ref. pg 117)
3. Deep fry sweet or chili pepper, sprinkle with salt and serve.

Koushari

Ingredients:
1 cup brown lentils
1 cup short grain rice
1 cup small elbow pasta
4 finely sliced onions
4 tablespoons olive oil

Method:
1. In 3 medium pans, boil the lentils, rice and pasta until cooked. Drain and keep aside.
2. Heat the oil in a frying pan, fry the onion until golden then remove from heat and drain on a kitchen towel.
3. In a serving plate, layer pasta, rice then lentils on top. Sprinkle the onions.

Sauce:

Ingredients:
1 whole garlic bulb
2 tablespoons tomato paste
2 cups water
2 tablespoons olive oil
Sprinkle of salt
Sprinkle of white pepper
¼ teaspoon chili powder
1 tablespoon cumin powder

Method:
1. Heat oil in a small pan, add garlic until golden, stir in tomato paste, cumin, salt, pepper, chili and water.
2. Boil for 10 mins, remove from heat and pour over lentil mixture.
3. Serve it cold or hot.

Eggplant with Tomato (Mousakaa)

Ingredients:
4 large eggplants
50g cooked chickpeas
300g fresh tomato puree
2 thinly sliced onions
3 cloves crushed garlic
1 thinly sliced green capsicum
2 cups water
1/3 teaspoon olive oil
1 teaspoon salt
¼ teaspoon white pepper
¼ teaspoon cinnamon powder
Sprinkle of sugar

Method:
1. Peel the eggplants and slice them to wedges. Soak in water for 25 minutes. Deep fry until golden. Remove from heat and drain on a kitchen towel.
2. In a medium pan heat the olive oil, fry the onions and garlic until soft adding all the seasonings with tomato puree and water. Simmer for 10 minutes.
3. Add chickpeas, capsicum and sugar then simmer for 2 minutes. Combine eggplants with the sauce and simmer for 5 minutes. Remove from heat.
4. Place eggplants in a deep serving plate. Serve cold with Lebanese bread.

Pumpkin Kibbé

Ingredients:
1 kg Pumpkin
300g fine cracked wheat
5 tablespoons finely chopped fresh coriander
4 grated medium onions
2 tablespoons finely chopped fresh mint basil
1 ½ cups plain flour
Pinch of salt
Pinch of cinnamon
Pinch of sweet pepper

Method:
1. Peel the pumpkin and cut it to chunks. Place it in a pan and boil to soften. Drain and squeeze out extra water and leave aside.
2. Soak the cracked wheat in a bowl of boiling water and leave for 10 minutes then squeeze out extra water and add over pumpkin.
3. In a large bowl, add the pumpkin, cracked wheat, flour, seasonings and coriander. Knead to a non-sticky dough.

Filling:

Ingredients:
5 finely sliced medium onions
½ a cup raisins
¼ cup olive oil
500g finely chopped silver beet or spinach
Sprinkle of salt
Sprinkle of sweet pepper

Method:
1. In medium frying pan heat the oil and fry the onions and raisins until the onions are soft. Add the seasonings and stir well.
2. Boil silver beet or spinach until soft. Drain and squeeze out water. Add over the onion mixture. Combine well and remove from heat to cool.

Method:
1. Brush an oven tray with oil and place ½ the pumpkin mixture into a thin layer. Place the filling on top.
2. Add the second layer of pumpkin mixture and press well. Use a knife to carve shapes. Pour olive oil on top, bake in a hot oven for around 40 minutes until golden brown. Serve cold or hot.

Okra with Tomato (Bamya)

Ingredients:
900g fresh or frozen okra
100g chopped fresh coriander
5 cloves crushed garlic
5 mashed tomatoes
3 cups water
¼ cup olive oil
4 tablespoons pomegranate molasses
Sprinkle of salt
Sprinkle of black pepper
Sprinkle of cinnamon

Method:
1. Cut the okra tips. Wash well then pat dry and fry until lightly golden using canola oil.
2. In large pan heat the oil and fry the garlic and coriander until the garlic is soft. Add the tomatoes, molasses, seasonings and water then boil for 5 minutes.
3. Add okra and simmer for 40 minutes until okra is soft and the sauce is lightly thick. Serve with Lebanese bread.

Note: Fry fresh okra before using.

Dan's Couscous

Ingredients:
1 small cabbage sliced thick
3 chopped onions
5 garlic cloves crushed
3 carrots chopped
2 medium sweet potatoes chopped
300g pumpkin chopped
5 zucchinis sliced in half in length
3 eggplants sliced in half in length
3 tomatoes chopped
4 cups vegetable stock
½ a cup olive oil
1 tablespoon Tabasco sauce
2 bay leaves
1 nutmeg flower
1 ½ teaspoons salt
1 tablespoon sweet paprika powder
¼ teaspoon Moroccan spices
2 tablespoons flour

Note: Moroccan spice is Ras el Hanout

Method:
1. Heat the oil in a large pan, cook onions and garlic until soft. Add carrots, zucchini, eggplants, sweet potatoes and tomatoes. Combine with stock and simmer at low heat.
2. Add all the seasonings with bay leaves and nutmeg flower. Stir until the vegetables are almost soft. Add pumpkin pieces and simmer for 10 minutes.
3. Mix the flour with ¼ cup cold water. Add to the mixture in a thin stream while stirring until bubbles slightly start forming and as the sauce thickens then remove from heat.

Couscous:

Ingredients:
500g couscous
1 tablespoon butter
Boiling water or stock
1 teaspoon salt

Method:
In a bowl, mix the couscous with all the ingredients, cover and leave for 20 minutes. Use a fork to fluff, then place the couscous in a serving plate topped with vegetables.

Potato Kibbé

Ingredients:
500g potatoes
¼ cup fine cracked wheat
1 grated onion
10 finely chopped fresh mint leaves
Sprinkle of salt
Sprinkle of white pepper

Method:
1. Cook the potatoes in a pan of boiling water until soft. Drain and mash until smooth. Place in a bowl and add seasonings, mint and grated onions then mix well.
2. In a small bowl add boiling water to cracked wheat and soak for 10 minutes. Drain and squeeze out excess water. Add to mashed potatoes and knead well to a soft dough.
3. Place the mix in a serving plate and press lightly to smooth the surface, drizzle with olive oil and serve with Lebanese bread and olives.

Zucchini Cakes

Ingredients:
6 grated zucchini
2 finely chopped onions
2 finely chopped tomatoes
½ a cup chopped fresh parsley
¼ cup chopped fresh mint
2 sliced green chilies
3 eggs
Oil for frying
1 cup plain flour
1 teaspoon salt
¼ teaspoon pepper
½ a teaspoon cinnamon
½ a teaspoon sweet pepper
1 teaspoon baking powder

Method:
1. In a bowl combine zucchinis, onions, tomatoes, parsley, mint, chili and all the seasonings then mix well.
2. Whisk the eggs in a small bowl. Add the flour and pour over the vegetables. Mix the whole very well, using a large wooden spoon until well combined.
3. Heat oil in a frying pan over medium heat. Drop in 2 tablespoons of the mixture and cook until the lower side is golden. Turn the cakes and cook on the other side. Drain on absorbent paper. Serve hot or cold.

Potato Cubes

Ingredients:
500g potatoes
¼ cup finely chopped fresh coriander
4 cloves crushed garlic
5 tablespoons lemon juice
¼ cup olive
Sprinkle of salt
Sprinkle of white pepper

Method:
1. Cut potatoes into 2cm cubes, deep fry in heated oil. Drain on absorbent paper and leave inside.
2. Heat olive oil in frying pan, cook garlic and coriander until lightly golden. Remove from heat and pour the mixture in a bowl.
3. Add lemon juice and seasonings. Stir well, combine potato and garlic with lemon juice and toss well and Mix. Serve cold.

Vegetable Stew

Ingredients:
2 large zucchinis
1 large potato
2 finely chopped tomatoes
2 carrots
1 cup green beans
1 cup kernel corn
2 finely chopped onions
3 cups water
3 tablespoons oil
Sprinkle of salt
Sprinkle of pepper
Sprinkle of cinnamon
Sprinkle of sweet pepper

Method:
1. Cut all the vegetables into 1cm cubes and leave aside.
2. Heat oil in a large pan and cook onions until soft. Add tomatoes, water and seasonings then boil for 5 minutes.
3. Add the vegetables and simmer at low heat until cooked. Serve with plain rice.

Note: In step 2, add 300g mince meat.

Sliced Potato (Miharaasa)

Ingredients:
500g sliced potatoes
5 sliced onions
½ a cup olive oil
Sprinkle of salt

Method:
1. Heat the oil in a deep frying pan. Cook onions until soft and caramelized. Add potatoes and keep stirring until soft.
2. Season with salt and combine well until potatoes become golden in color. Place in a plate and serve cold or hot with Lebanese bread.

Panchit with vegetables

Ingredients:
300g peeled raw prawns (optional)
200g boiled and shredded chicken (optional)
4 finely sliced medium onions
1 finely sliced clove garlic
2 medium carrots peeled sliced
2 finely chopped celery sticks
2 cups finely shredded cabbage
100g green beans cut in length
¼ cup soy sauce
250g vermicelli jumbo
1 teaspoon grated ginger
Sprinkle of salt
1 teaspoon freshly grated black pepper

Method:
1. In a bowl pour boiling water over the vermicelli and soak them for 5 to10 minutes and drain them.
2. Heat the oil in a large pan, add garlic and stir until lightly browned. Place the onions and cook until soft.
3. Add prawns and vegetables to combine well with soy sauce, black pepper and sprinkle of salt. Stir for 3 minutes and remove from heat. Vegetables should be crunchy.
4. Add the vermicelli and toss well. Place back over heat and cook for 3 minutes while stirring. Serve hot, garnished with slice of lemon.

Potato and Zucchini

Ingredients:
1 large potato
4 zucchinis
1 finely chopped tomato
2 cloves crushed garlic
1 finely chopped small onion
¼ cup olive oil
Sprinkle of salt
Sprinkle of white pepper

Method:
1. Cut potato and zucchinis into 1cm cubes. Sprinkle salt on top and leave aside.
2. Heat the oil in a large pan, cook the onion and garlic while stirring until soft then add potato and zucchinis.
3. Add the tomato and seasonings with ½ a cup of water and cook until the potato is soft. Simmer for 5 more minutes then remove from heat.
4. Place the mixture in a deep serving plate. Serve cold with Lebanese bread.

Pat's Potato

Ingredients:
4 sliced large potatoes
4 cloves crushed garlic
3 eggs
1 tablespoon flour
1 ½ cups cheddar cheese
150g cream
1 cup milk
5 tablespoons butter
1 teaspoon salt
½ a teaspoon white pepper
½ a teaspoon grated nutmeg

Method:
1. In a deep oven plate, place the potatoes in layers and leave aside.
2. In a bowl whisk eggs, milk, flour and seasonings well. Melt the butter in a medium pan, cook garlic until light gold and add to the egg mixture combining well.
3. Stir over medium heat until the sauce thickens. Remove from heat, add the cream and combine well
4. Pour the sauce over the potatoes and sprinkle cheese on top.
5. Bake until golden and serve hot.

Mashed Potato

Ingredients:
500g potatoes
1 ½ cups milk
50g butter
1 teaspoon salt

Method:
1. Cook potatoes in a pan of boiling water until soft. Drain and peel the skins off then mash until smooth.
2. Add butter, salt and milk. Combine well until the mixture becomes smooth and creamy. Serve hot.

Mash potato with cheese

1. Follow the same procedure to prepare the mashed potatoes
2. Grease a shallow dish, place half of the mashed potatoes quantity, sprinkle 300g of grated mozzarella or cheddar.
3. Top with another layer of mashed potatoes, drizzle with melted butter. Bake uncovered until bubbling and golden.

Stuffed Mushroom

Ingredients:
6 large fresh mushrooms
1 sliced medium tomato
½ a teaspoon mustard
2 eggs
½ a cup milk
1 cup fresh breadcrumbs
6 thin slices cheddar cheese
½ a cup grated cheddar cheese

Method:
1. Remove stems from the mushrooms, finely slice and combine with mustard, grated cheese and breadcrumbs.
2. In a medium bowl whisk eggs and milk then combine with grated cheese.
3. Stuff the mushrooms with the filling and top with sliced cheese and tomato.
4. Place the stuffed mushrooms on an oven tray and bake until cheese melts.

Sweet Potato

Ingredients:
500g sweet potatoes
30g butter
1 cup milk
6 tablespoons sugar

Method:
1. Cook the potatoes in a pan of boiling water until soft. Drain and peel the skins off then mash until smooth.
2. Add butter, sugar and milk. Combine well to a smooth creamy mixture.
3. Place the mixture in a deep oven dish, smooth the top and drizzle with melted butter. Bake uncovered until bubbling. Serve hot or warm.

Stuffed Tomatoes

Ingredients:
5 large tomatoes cut in halves
5 boiled eggs
4 tablespoons cheddar cheese
2 tablespoons mayonnaise
Salt and black pepper to season

Method:
1. Cut the top of the tomato.
2. Use a spoon to carefully scoop out the flesh and keep aside.
3. In a medium bowl, use a fork to mash the eggs well then combine, cheese, mayonnaise and seasonings.
4. Spoon the filling into the tomato halves and top with slices of gherkins. Arrange the tomatoes on a serving plate and serve cold.

Mixed Stuffed Vegetables

Ingredients:
500g small size zucchinis
300g small size eggplants
300g medium size firm tomatoes
200g medium size capsicums
200g medium size onions

Filling

Ingredients:
500g short grain rice
1 cup finely chopped fresh parsley
3 finely chopped onions
2 tablespoons tomato paste
6 cups water or vegetable stock
¼ cup olive oil
¼ cup lemon juice
Sprinkle of salt
Sprinkle of white pepper
Sprinkle of sweet pepper

Method:
1. Use a corer to hollow the zucchinis and eggplants.
2. Place the onions in boiling water for 10 minutes, drain, hollow their center and finely chop the inner flesh.
3. Cut the top of a tomato and scoop out its flesh using a spoon.
4. Heat the oil in a medium pan and cook the onions until soft. Add the rice and stir for 5 minutes then combine tomatoes, paste and seasonings. Stir for 5 minutes then remove from heat.
5. Add lemon juice, parsley and combine well. Stuff the vegetables with the mixture.
6. Place the vegetables in a large pan and press them with a plate on top to keep them in a place. Cover with water, boil, then reduce heat and simmer over low heat for 50 to 60 minutes.
7. Remove from heat and lift out the vegetables with a slotted spoon. Place in a serving plate.

Baked Capsicum

Ingredients:
5 small red capsicums
5 tablespoons cream
5 eggs
½ a cup grated cheddar cheese
Salt and black pepper to season

Method:
1. Cut the top of the capsicums, remove the core and seeds and season the inside.
2. Place them in an oven dish.
3. Break an egg in each capsicum, top with cream and cheese.
4. Bake for 20 minutes until the egg is cooked.
Serve hot.

Note: Use ripe tomatoes instead of capsicums.

Lubya Bil Zeit

Ingredients:
500g green beans
2 finely sliced onions
2 cloves crushed garlic
500g finely chopped tomatoes
½ a cup water
½ a cup olive oil
Salt and pepper to season

Method:
1. Trim the green beans and remove any strings then wash under cold water and drain well.
2. Heat then oil in a medium pan, add garlic and onions to cook until soft and lightly gold. Add the beans and toss them together with onions.
3. Add the tomatoes and cook for 10 minutes until soft. Season to taste and combine with water. Stir occasionally until green beans are soft and the sauce thickens. Remove from heat.
4. Place the green beans in a deep serving plate. Serve cold with Lebanese bread.

Vegetarian Burger

Ingredients:
1 cup cracked wheat
¾ cup dry chickpeas
1 cup plain flour
3 medium finely chopped onions
½ a cup finely chopped fresh parsley
½ a cup finely chopped fresh mint
¼ cup finely chopped fresh coriander
Sprinkle of chili powder
Salt and black pepper to season

Method:
1. Soak the chickpeas in a bowl of water overnight. Drain and place in a food processor.
2. Soak cracked wheat in a bowl of hot water for 10 minutes, drain and squeeze out extra water. Place over the chickpeas in the food processor.
3. Process while adding the herbs and seasonings until the mixture forms a rough paste. Remove and place the mixture in a bowl, add the flour and knead well using damp hands and divide the mixture into 4 to 6 large patties. Refrigerate for 15 minutes then shallow fry over medium heat on each side until golden. Serve with green salad.

Burgal AA Banadoura

Ingredients:
500g diced red tomato
2 cups burghul
2 finely chopped onions
5 cloves crushed garlic
¼ cup olive oil
½ a cup water water
½ a teaspoon black and sweet pepper (all spices) to season
1 teaspoon salt

Method:
1. Soak burghul in a bowl of warm water for 10 minutes then drain well.
2. Heat oil in a medium pan, cook onions until soft. Add tomato puree, water and seasonings, boil for 5 minutes.
3. Add burghul and simmer on low heat, stirring occasionally until cooked and sauce is creamy. Remove from heat, combine garlic in burghul.
4. Place the mixture in a deep serving plate. Serve cold.

Altisha

Ingredients:
3 medium thinly sliced onions
4 thinly sliced carrots
2 sliced potatoes
1 capsicum cut into thin strips
1 fresh chili
½ a teaspoon fresh Rosemarie
½ a cup water
¼ cup oil
1 teaspoon salt

Method:
1. Heat the oil in a medium pan. Cook the onions and carrots until soft, add potato slices and fold gently.
2. Add capsicum, chili, salt and water. Simmer at low heat for around 7 minutes. Remove from heat and stir in the Rosemarie leaves. Serve hot or cold.

Fasoulia Bil Zeit

Ingredients:
2 cups dry beans
2 finely chopped onions
4 garlic cloves
2 finely sliced green chilies
2 finely chopped tomatoes
¼ cup olive oil
1 cup water
1 bay leaf
Salt and black pepper to season

Method:
1. Soak beans in a bowl of water over night. Drain well and place in a pan of water with the bay leaf. Boil uncovered until soft. Drain and keep aside.
2. Heat the oil in a pan, cook onions until golden. Add garlic, chilies, tomatoes, water and seasonings. Simmer at low heat for 8 minutes. Combine with the boiled beans and toss well.
3. Remove from heat and place all in a deep serving plate. Serve cold with Lebanese bread.

Sogo

Ingredients:
5 finely chopped onions
4 cloves crushed garlic
1 tablespoon grated fresh ginger
2 red tomatoes
2 boiled eggs
1 can tuna (optional)
2 potatoes cut into small fried cubes (optional)
½ a tablespoon fresh Rosemarie leaves
½ a cup water
¼ cup oil
Salt and pepper to season
Cinnamon powder and cumin powder to season
1 tablespoon of Barbari (Ethiopian spices)

Method:
1. Heat the oil in a medium pan and cook onions until golden. Add garlic, ginger, tomato puree, water and all the seasonings.
2. Boil for 5 minutes then simmer at low heat. Add the eggs and simmer until sauce thickens. Combine Rosemarie leaves, tuna and potato.
3. Serve with boiled pasta or bread.

Sea Food

Sea foods are God's way to show us how much he loves us, just to be able to have that variety of sizes, colors, and shapes to taste is just out of this world, and not to forget the benefits and oils they provide us with.

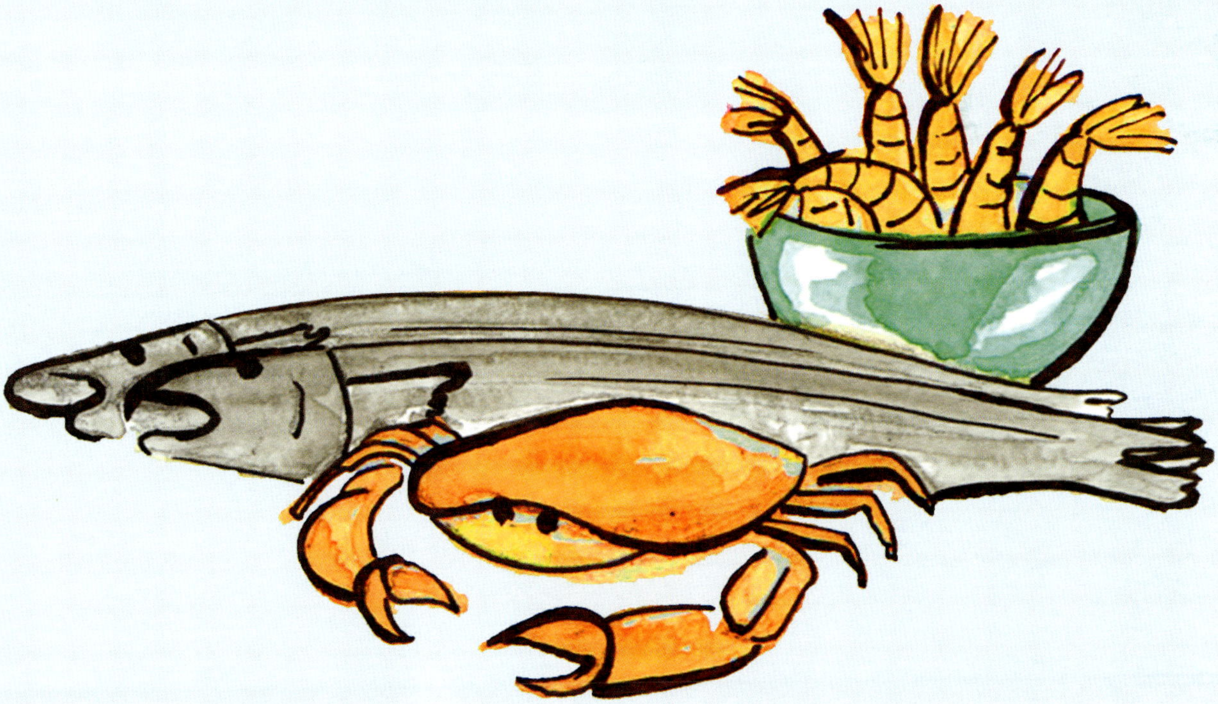

Pan Fried Fish

Ingredients:
5 firm fish (Snapper-Sea bass-Groper)
1 cup oil for shallow frying
3 tablespoons plain flour
Sprinkle of salt

Method:
1. Sift flour and salt onto a dinner plate. Coat both sides of the fish with seasoned flour.
2. Heat oil in a medium frying pan and place the fish to cook for 4 to 5 minutes on each side, then turn and cook the other side.
3. Remove fish from pan and drain on paper towels.

Tahini sauce:

Ingredients:
¼ cup Tahini
2 tablespoons chopped parsley
½ a cup lemon juice
½ a cup water
1 teaspoon salt

Method:
1. In a large bowl place Tahini, lemon juice, water and salt. Mix to form a thin sauce (may need extra water). Combine parlsey in.
2. Place the fried fish on the serving plate with lemon wedges on the side and deep fried Lebanese bread. Serve with the Tahini Sauce.

Fish Patties

Ingredients:
700g skinless fish fillet (groper-snapper)
1 egg
2 tablespoons plain flour
1 finely chopped small onion
4 tablespoons finely chopped fresh coriander
1 boiled medium potato
Pinch of turmeric
Pinch of ground curry leaves
Pinch of cumin powder
Sprinkle of salt
Sprinkle of pepper

Method:
1. Remove any bones from the fish. Combine 2 ½ cups of water with 1 bay leaf in a large pan and boil. Add the fish and poach for 5 to 7 minutes until cooked. Remove the fish, flake it and keep aside.
2. In a large bowl mash the potato using a fork. Combine the coriander, onion, flour and egg. Knead well.
3. Add all the seasonings with the flaked fish. Combine well and leave aside for 30 minutes.
4. Divide the mixture into 8 to 10 patties and coat lightly with flour. Fry in heated oil in a frying pan. Cook 2 to 3 minutes on each side until golden. Drain and serve hot.

Baked Groper

Ingredients:
1 kg whole groper scaled and gutted
2 thinly sliced lemons
2 thinly sliced onions
2 teaspoons oil
½ a teaspoon salt
Sprinkle of pepper

Method:
1. Fill the cavity of the fish with ½ of the sliced lemons and onions. Sprinkle with salt and pepper. Drizzle oil on top then cover with the rest of the sliced onions and lemons.
2. Wrap the fish completely with aluminum foil and place into a deep-sided baking dish. Bake for 30 to 40 minutes until cooked.
3. Remove the fish from the aluminum foil and transfer to a serving dish. Serve with green salad. (Ref. pg 25)

Spicy fish with Vegetables

Ingredients:
1 ½ kg whole fish (snapper)
2 sliced onions
¼ cup lemon juice
1/3 cup olive oil
3 finely chopped green capsicums
¼ cup chopped fresh coriander
3 cloves crushed garlic
¼ cup toasted pine nuts
2 teaspoons salt
½ a teaspoon red chili pepper
2 green chilies sliced
3 tomatoes chopped finely

Method:
1. Place the fish in a large baking dish. Bake in a hot oven for 40 minutes until the fish is cooked. Remove from the oven and place on a serving plate.
2. Heat the oil in a medium bowl, place onions and stir until golden. Add garlic, capsicums, chilies, tomatoes, coriander and seasonings. Stir well until it forms a thick sauce. Remove from heat.
3. Spoon the mixture over the fish and sprinkle the pine nuts. Serve with Lebanese bread.

Baby shark and Spices

Ingredients:
1 kg whole baby shark or groper
5 finely chopped onions
3 garlic cloves crushed
4 finely chopped red tomatoes
½ a cup oil
1 tablespoon mixed pepper
½ a tablespoon dried lime powder
2 tablespoons turmeric

Note: Use 2 cans of tuna instead

Method:
1. Slice the baby shark into 4 to 5 pieces, place in a large pan of boiling water and poach for 5 to 10 minutes until cooked. Drain well and put the stock aside.
2. Remove any bone from the baby shark, flake the meat and keep aside.
3. In the same pan, heat the oil, add the onions and stir until browned. Stir in the dried lime powder, turmeric, mixed pepper and garlic. Cook well.
4. Add tomatoes and baby shark flakes to combine well. Add up about 1 cup from the stock then cover the pan and simmer at low heat for 20 to 25 minutes. Remove from heat and place in a serving plate.

Spicy fish

Ingredients:
1 ½ kg whole groper
1 clove crushed garlic
2 ½ cups walnuts
4 green chilies
200g chopped fresh coriander
½ a cup Tahini
¼ cup lemon juice
1 ½ cups water
½ a cup oil
½ a teaspoon cinnamon powder
1 ½ teaspoons salt
1 teaspoon sweet pepper

Method:
1. Make 3 to 4 diagonal slits on both sides of the fish. Heat the oven and place the fish in a large baking dish. Bake for 40 minutes until cooked then remove from oven, leave to cool. Flake the fish and remove the bones then aside.
2. In a food processor place the walnuts and process until obtaining a fine powder. Remove from processor and place coriander, garlic and chilies then process until finely chopped.
3. In large pan, heat oil and fry the garlic mixture and coriander until soft. Add walnuts and combine well.
4. Stir in water, lemon juice, Tahini and seasonings stirring frequently until sauce boils and thickens. Remove from heat and leave to cool.
5. Place the flaked fish in a deep serving plate and cover the top with sauce. Serve it cold with Lebanese bread.

Stuffed Squid

Ingredients:
10 small squids
1 cup boiled short grain rice
4 cloves crushed garlic
1 finely chopped stem lemongrass
5 tablespoons finely chopped fresh coriander
2 teaspoons green curry paste
2 tablespoons fish sauce
2 tablespoons rice flour
1 tablespoon soya sauce
1 tablespoon water
1 tablespoon oil
2 teaspoons sugar

Method:
1. Clean the squids without removing their tips. Wash the tubes well.
2. Heat the oil in a large pan, add garlic, lemongrass, coriander and curry paste. Stir to fry for 3 minutes. Add fish sauce, boiled rice and rice flour then mix well.
3. Fill each squid with the mixture and secure the end with toothpick.
4. In a medium bowl combine soya sauce, water and sugar. Place the squids in secure side up position. Leave for 5 to 10 minutes.
5. In a large frying pan brush it with oil and heat the pan. Add the squids, turning frequently until firm. Leave for 5 minutes before slicing.
6. Serve with sweet chili sauce.

Squid with Ink

Ingredients:
1 kg squid
2 whole diced tomatoes
2 finely chopped onions
4 cloves crushed garlic
2 finely sliced green chilies
1/3 cup vinegar
¼ cup soya sauce
½ a teaspoon black pepper

Method:
1. Clean the squids and keep the ink bags aside.
2. Gently pull the tentacles. The intestine should come away simultaneously. Cut the tentacles under the eyes then remove the beak and gently pull away the soft bone and the ink bay that is attached to the intestines and put aside.
3. Rub the hoods under cold running water. The skin should come out easily. Slice the squid into rings then wash and drain well.
4. Heat the oil in a medium pan. Place the onions and garlic then stir until soft. Add tomatoes and pepper and keep stirring to obtain a thick sauce. At boiling point, place the squid and the ink bag and smash it with a spoon. Cook for 3 minutes.
5. Add vinegar, soya sauce and chilies then boil for 2 minutes. Serve with plain rice or pasta.

Cham Prawn

Ingredients:
700g large raw prawns
500g boiled spaghetti
300g bacon
1 clove crushed garlic
60g butter
4 cups cream
½ a cup water
Sprinkle of salt
Sprinkle of pepper

Method:
1. In a medium bowl, place the prawns with ½ a cup lemon juice, salt and pepper. Let aside for a half hour.
2. Toast bacon in a frying pan until crispy then remove and place on a plate to cool. Slice to small bites.
3. Heat butter in a medium pan, fry garlic until golden, put the whole prawns and stir for 3 minutes until their color changes.
4. Add cream, water, salt and pepper. Stir until heated then sprinkle bacon over it and stir for 1 additional minute. Serve the sauce on top of pasta.

Tuna Burger

Ingredients:
500g skinless tuna fillet
3 Hamburger buns split in half
2 sliced tomatoes
1 lettuce leaf
2 finely chopped spring onions
1 finely chopped green chili
2 tablespoons finely chopped fresh coriander
2 tablespoons mayonnaise
Plain flour for dusting
Sprinkle of salt
Sprinkle of pepper

Note: Use 500g salmon fillet.

Method:
1. In a large bowl combine onions, chili, coriander, mayonnaise, salt and pepper.
2. Process tuna fillet in a food processor until roughly minced.
3. Add tuna over the mixture and mix well using your hands. Shape into 3 to 4 patties. Dust with flour and refrigerate for an hour.
4. Heat the oil in a large pan, add the patties and cook until browned on each side.
5. Grill the buns on each base. Add some lettuce, tomatoes for each burger and some mayonnaise or tartar sauce on top.

Crab with Mustard Seeds

Ingredients:
6 medium raw crabs
2 finely chopped onions
4 cloves crushed garlic
2 chopped red chilies
½ a cup chopped fresh coriander
½ a cup tomato puree
1 cup coconut milk
3 tablespoons oil
2 tablespoons mustard seeds
1 tablespoon grated ginger
1 teaspoon curry powder
Sprinkle of salt

Method:
1. Pull the crab shells away from the body. Wash very well.
2. Heat the oil in a medium pan. Add the onions, garlic, ginger and chilies. Stir over heat until onions are soft.
3. Add mustard seeds, coriander, tomato and coconut milk then simmer at low heat for 5 minutes.
4. Add the crab to the sauce, sprinkle salt and simmer for 10 minutes while turning the crabs around until cooked. Serve hot.

Tajin

Ingredients:
1 can tuna or baked flaked fish
1 finely chopped onion
¼ cup Tahini
2 tablespoons oil
¼ cup lemon juice
½ a cup water
2 tablespoons toasted pine nuts
½ a teaspoon salt

Method:
1. Heat the oil in a medium pan. Stir in the onion until soft. Add Tahini, lemon juice, water and salt stirring frequently until the sauce boils and thickens.
2. Place the fish over the mixture and stir for 2 minutes. Remove it from heat spoon it in a deep serving plate. Sprinkle the pine nuts and serve it cold with Pita bread.

Lobster with Cheese

Ingredients:
1 cooked lobster
1 chopped large onion
2 bay leaves
60g butter
4 tablespoons plain flour
1 tablespoon mustard
1 cup of grated cheddar cheese
2 tablespoons grated Parmesan cheese
3 cups milk

Method:
1. Cut the lobster in half, in length. Remove the vein and as much meat as possible then keep aside.
2. In a medium pan combine milk, onion and bay leaves. Bring to boil for 5 minutes then remove from heat and ladle the stock into a sieve over a bowl.
3. Melt butter in a pan, stir in flour until it bubbles gradually then add the hot milk stirring constantly until it boils and thickens. Remove from heat and add cheddar cheese and mustard.
4. Add lobster meat to the cheese mixture and spoon the mixture into the lobster shell. Sprinkle Parmesan cheese and place under a hot grill until the cheese is lightly golden. Serve hot.

Prawn Tempura

Ingredients:
Peel the prawns leaving the tail and combine with crushed garlic.
Season with black pepper, salt and grated ginger.

Method:
In a bowl whisk 2 cups of water, 1 egg, 1 ¼ cup of flour or rice flour and mix to a heavy dip.

Dip the prawns in the mix and deep fry until golden.

Tuna with Lettuce

Ingredients:
1 can tuna
1 whole sliced lettuce
2 finely chopped tomatoes
2 finely chopped onions
8 cloves crushed garlic
¼ cup water
4 tablespoons oil
¼ cup soya sauce
Sprinkle of salt
Sprinkle of Ajinomoto

Method:
1. Heat the oil and the tuna oil in a large pan, cook garlic until browned lightly then add the onions and cook until soft.
2. Add tomatoes and stir until all is well combined. Place flaked tuna water, soya sauce and lettuce and toss until well combined. Simmer at low heat for 2 minutes.
3. Sprinkle salt and Ajinomoto while tossing well. Remove from heat and serve with plain rice.

Cham tajin

Ingredients:
- 1 ½ kg whole cleaned Gropper fish
- 3 cups Basmati rice
- ½ a cup lemon juice
- 7 finely chopped onions
- 2 sliced crispy fried onions
- 1 garlic clove crushed
- 3 finely chopped tomatoes
- 2 teaspoons lime powder
- 2 teaspoons cumin powder
- 1 tablespoon mixed spices (Bizar)
- 2 teaspoons sugar
- 1 teaspoon salt

Method:
1. In a medium bowl whisk lemon juice, lime powder, black pepper, cumin and salt. Cut the fish into equal pieces and soak in the lemon mixture for 30 minutes.
2. Heat the oil in a large pan and cook the onion and garlic until browned lightly. Add tomatoes and sugar and stir well. Remove 4 tablespoons of the mixture and keep aside.
3. In a large pan fry fish on both sides until cooked and add 6 cups of water. Simmer then remove fish and pour the stock over the rice to cook.
4. Add rice over the mixture then combine with mixed spices, salt and fish sauce. Simmer at low heat stirring occasionally until the rice is cooked.
5. Serve the rice on the serving plate topped with fish and sprinkle the crispy onions on the side.

Sauce: Place the 4 tablespoons of tomato mixture in a small pan and add 1 cup of water and 1 finely chopped tomato, salt and chili powder (optional). Boil while stirring until it becomes a thick sauce. Serve separately with the rice.

Fish Kibbé

Ingredients:
500g white skinless fish fillet
1 cup fine cracked wheat
1 whole lemon zest
2 small grated onions
¼ cup finely chopped fresh coriander
½ a white pepper
1 teaspoon salt

Filling:

Ingredients:
4 finely sliced onions
¼ cup pine nuts
¼ cup olive oil
4 tablespoons olive oil extra
1 teaspoon salt
½ a teaspoon black pepper
3 saffron threads

Method:
1. In a medium bowl soak the cracked wheat for 15 minutes, drain well, and retrieve the extra water absorbed by the wheat.
2. In a food processor place the fish fillet, lemon zest, onions, coriander and seasoning then process until well combined.
3. While processing, add the cracked wheat and process for 10 seconds. Transfer the mixture to a bowl. Refrigerate for at least 30 minutes.

Method:
1. Heat the oil in a large frying pan and cook the onions until soft. Add the pine nuts and all the seasonings then stir well for a minute and remove from heat.
2. Place the onion mixture at the bottom of a baking tray. Spread well and add the fish mixture on top. Press well to level the surface then add the olive oil extra and slice the top to medium squares.
3. Bake in a hot oven for around 30 minutes until cooked. Remove from oven and serve cold.

Tuna Kofta

Ingredients:
1 can tuna
2 medium grated potatoes
3 grated carrots
2 grated celery sticks
1 cup grated green beans
2 cubes chicken stock
¼ cup oil
Plain flour for dusting

Method:
1. Heat the oil in a medium pan, fry the chicken cubes until they melt and add the potatoes then stir until cooked.
2. Add the rest of the vegetables. Stir until well combined and cooked. Remove from heat, add tuna and mash the whole with a fork then leave aside.
3. Shape the mixture into ovals using a rounded tablespoon, toss in flour and remove excess flour.
4. Shallow-fry the kofta ovals in hot oil until browned lightly then drain on absorbent paper. Serve hot.

Poultry

As one of the most domestic and widespread animals, chickens have a multifunctional use in man's life. Back when it was used as trade between households, the eggs it lays or its delicious different body parts we can enjoy deep fried, breaded or grilled.

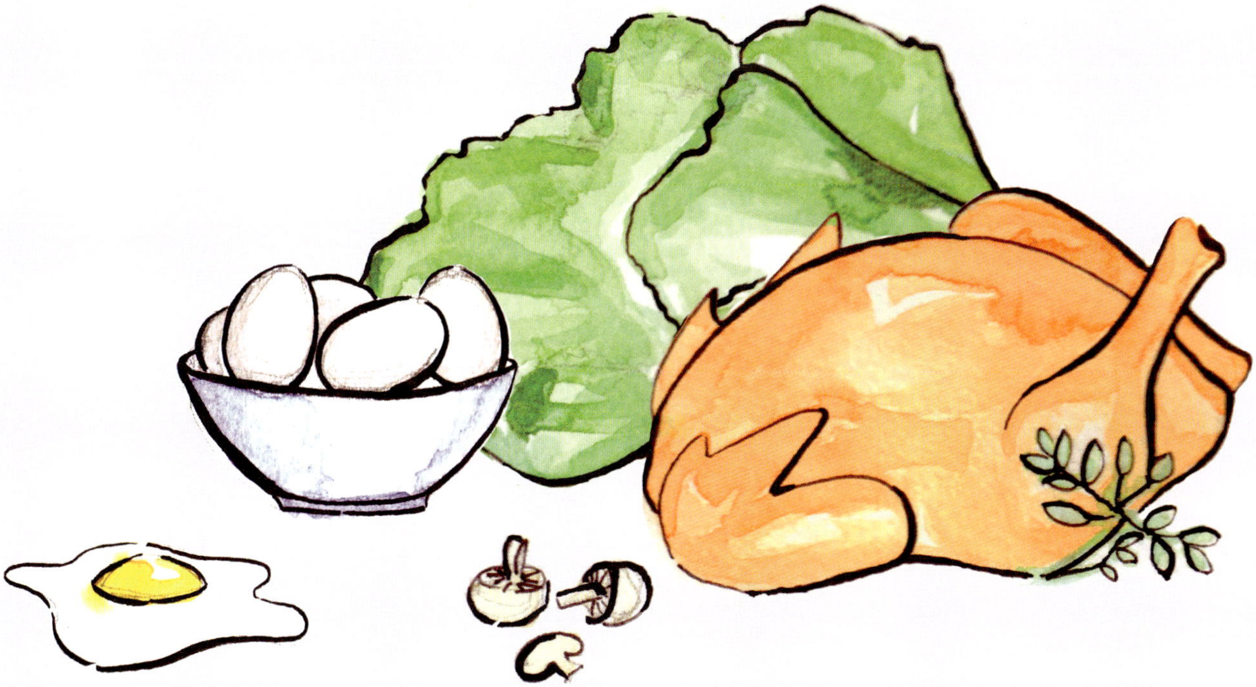

Shish Tawou

Ingredients:
1kg chicken breast cut into cubes
¼ cup olive oil
¼ cup lemon juice
9 crushed cloves garlic
½ a teaspoon white pepper

Method 1:
1. Whisk oil, lemon juice, garlic, salt and pepper well. Combine chicken and toss well.
2. Cover with plastic wrap in the refrigerator overnight. Place them in a baking dish, bake in a hot oven until cooked stirring occasionally.
3. Or thread chicken into skewers on a grill or barbecue stand until tender and well browned, turning often. Serve with garlic dip (Ref. pg 18).

Method 2:
Marinate chicken in:
2 tablespoons ketchup
¼ cup lemon juice
4 tablespoons mayonnaise
1 tablespoon French mustard
4 cloves crushed garlic
1 tablespoon oil
Salt and black pepper to season

Chicken Pie

Ingredients:
500g boiled chicken
500g fresh spinach
200g sliced mushroom
2 finely chopped onions
250g cream
1 cup cheddar cheese
1 pack puff pastry
Salt and black pepper to season
Sprinkle of chopped fresh
Coriander

Method:
1. Cut the pastry in half and roll half of it on a lightly floured surface, large enough to cover base and sides of a greased flat tin.
2. Combine shredded chicken, spinach, mushroom, onion, cream, cheese, coriander, salt and pepper toss well.
3. Spoon the mixture into the prepared pastry case. Roll the second half of pastry on lightly floured surface, large enough to cover top of pie and press down the edges with fork to seal.
4. Bake in moderate oven for 45 minutes until golden brown. Serve hot.

Simple Roasted Chicken

Ingredients:
2 whole chickens
Salt to season

Method:
1. Sprinkle chicken with salt inside and outside.
2. Place them on a tray and bake in a hot oven until golden brown and crisp
3. Serve with garlic dip or mayonnaise. (Ref. pg 18)

Chicken With Potato

Ingredients:
1 whole chicken cut into quarters
4 large potatoes cut to cubes
5 cloves crushed garlic
1/3 cup lemon juice
Sprinkle of cinnamon
Sprinkle of black pepper
1 teaspoon salt

Method:
1. Stir garlic, lemon juice and seasonings in a bowl. Combine chicken and potatoes.
2. Place chicken in single layer in a shallow oven dish. Pour sauce and potatoes over.
3. Cover dish with aluminum foil .Bake for an hour turning occasionally. Remove aluminum and bake for 10 minutes until golden brown.

Chicken Tikkha

Ingredients:
2 whole chickens cut to quarters
2 cups yoghurt
10g fresh ginger
3 green chilies
2 whole cloves
4 whole cardamoms
½ a cup lemon juice
2 tablespoons oil
1 tablespoon sweet paprika
Sprinkle of cinnamon
Salt and black pepper to season

Method:
1. Place the chicken in a large bowl.
2. Add all the ingredients in a food processor and process until creamy.
3. Toss chicken with sauce, cover with plastic wrap in the refrigerator overnight. Barbecue or grill or bake.
4. Serve with bread.

Chicken Pancakes

Pancake Dough:

Ingredients:
2 eggs
½ a cup flour
¾ cup milk
2 tablespoons oil
1 teaspoon baking powder
Salt to season

Method:
1. Combine all in a bowl, whisk well to thin light cream dough.
2. Heat a non stick frying pan and pour some of dough swirl around to a thin pancake and light golden. Remove from pan and put aside, cover with towel.

Filling (Option 1)

Ingredients:
750g shredded boiled chicken
2 onions finely chopped
3 garlic cloves crushed
1 finely chopped tomato
1 tablespoon fresh chopped coriander
1 finely chopped red capsicum
1 tablespoon oil
Salt and soya sauce to season

Method:
1. Heat oil in a large pan cook onions, garlic until golden. Stir in tomato, capsicum, chicken, coriander, salt and soya sauce stir well and almost dry.
2. Place 2 tablespoons of filling in center of pancake and close the side. Fold the other side well. Toss in whisked egg then into breadcrumbs and fry in hot oil to golden brown.
3. Serve hot.

Filling (Option 2)

Ingredients:
500g precooked minced meat
1 cup grated cheddar cheese
1 finely chopped onion
1 tablespoon olive oil
1 cup kernel corn
½ a cup kidney beans
1 tablespoon tomato paste
Breadcrumbs
Chili powder and cumin powder to season
Salt and black pepper to season

Method:
1. Heat oil in a large pan and cook onion until soft.
2. Add meat, corn, beans, tomato paste and seasonings. Toss well.
3. Remove from heat.
4. Place 2 tablespoons of filling in the center of pancake, close the side. Roll to spring roll.
5. Toss in whisked egg then into breadcrumbs. Fry in a hot oil to golden brown.
6. Serve hot.

Chicken Burger

Ingredients:
800g minced chicken
2 chopped onions
1/3 cup cream cheese
2 cloves crushed garlic
1 tablespoon chopped fresh chives
7 Burger buns
Salt and black pepper to season

Method:
1. Using your hands, mix well together all the ingredients in a large bowl. Divide the mixture into 7 equal portions and shape into patties.
2. Add 1 tablespoon of oil in a frying pan cook the burger pressing slightly. Cook over medium heat until browned on both side.
3. Split the bun in half toast and slightly place a burger topped with sliced cheese, tomato, pickles and little mayonnaise.
4. Serve with French Fries.

Chicken With Honey

Ingredients:
2 whole chickens cut to 4 or 6 pieces
½ a cup honey
4 tablespoons soya Sauce
3 tablespoons teriyaki Sauce
Salt and black pepper to season

Method:
1. Combine honey, soya sauce, teriyaki, and seasonings in a bowl. Add chicken toss well.
2. Cover with plastic wrap. Refrigerate overnight and place in a baking dish.
3. Bake until golden brown. Add a cup of water while baking, turning occasionally.
4. Serve with rice or baked potato.

Chicken Adobo

Ingredients:
5 chicken drum sticks, ½ boiled
8 half boiled chicken wings
2 tablespoons oil
1 whole bulb garlic peeled and sliced
4 thinly sliced onions
3 sliced green chilies
½ a teaspoon black pepper
Salt and soya sauce to season
2 tablespoons vinegar
Sprinkle of Ajinomoto
(Ref. glossary)

Method:
1. Heat oil in large pan and cook garlic until browned. Add onions, chili, and black pepper. Stir well till the onions soften.
2. Add chicken, turning occasionally on medium heat for 5 to 10 minutes. Stir in the soya sauce and half a cup of water. Cook until chicken softens.
3. Remove from heat. Sprinkle Ajinomoto and vinegar. Stir well and serve hot with plain rice. (Ref. pg 108)

Baked Chicken wings

Ingredients:
12 chicken wings
12 garlic cloves
¼ cup olive oil
2 tablespoons chili sauce
½ a cup grated Parmesan
1 cup breadcrumbs
Black pepper to season

Method:
1. Add garlic, oil, chili sauce and pepper in a blender mixing to a paste. Pour in a bowl and add the cheese. Mix well.
2. Soak chicken wings in mixture for 2 hours. Remove from sauce and dip one at a time in breadcrumbs.
3. Bake in a hot oven until golden brown.
4. Remove from heat and place on a plate.

Abbzi Adoubo

Ingredients:
500g fresh mushrooms
5 sliced onions
8 drum sticks
2 chicken stock cubes
8 cloves sliced garlic
2 tablespoons soya sauce
1 tablespoon Teriyaki sauce
1 ½ cups water
1 ½ cups cream
2 tablespoons olive oil
2 green chilies
Salt to season
1 tablespoon paprika

Method:
1. Heat oil in a large pan, cook onions and mushrooms until tender. Remove from heat and spoon on a plate.
2. In the same pan add chicken stock cubes and stir with garlic, until the chicken turns golden. Add water and simmer on medium heat until chicken is tender.
3. Stir in sauces, salt, paprika, cream, chili and simmer on low heat until bubbles appear stirring occasionaly.
4. Remove from heat and serve with white rice.

Chicken Cordon Bleu

Ingredients:
5 chicken breast fillet
5 slices cheddar cheese
1 lightly beaten egg
½ a cup breadcrumbs
½ a cup flour
Oil for frying
Salt and black pepper to season

Method:
1. Cut into the thickest part of fillet without completely cutting through it. Open and season.
2. Place a slice cheese on one side of the opening. Fold the rest to enclose filling.
3. Coat with flour, dip into egg and coat in breadcrumbs.
4. Heat oil in a pan, place the chicken and cook over low heat until chicken is tender and golden. Serve hot with salad.

Chicken Liver

Ingredients:
1 kg chicken liver
5 garlic cloves crushed
½ a cup lemon juice
½ a cup fresh chopped coriander
2 tablespoons oil
Cinnamon to season
Salt and white pepper to season
3 tablespoons pomegranate molasses

Method:
1. Clean and wash livers, drain to dry.
2. Heat oil in a medium pan and cook liver folding occasionally until almost dry.
3. Combine garlic, lemon juice, coriander and seasonings and stir for a minute. add pomegranate.
4. Spoon the mix to a serving plate.
5. Serve with Lebanese bread.

Note: Fry livers with butter and crushed garlic. Season well.
Add 3 tablespoons of lemon juice and 4 tablespoons of Pomegranate molasses.
Serve hot.

Meats

Meat goes back to human's real nature, the hunt for his food and the adrenaline rush it gives him. Man's worse qualities came to surface when he stopped his hunting and gathering activities, but still the feeling he gets when his teeth are grazed into meat is sensational.

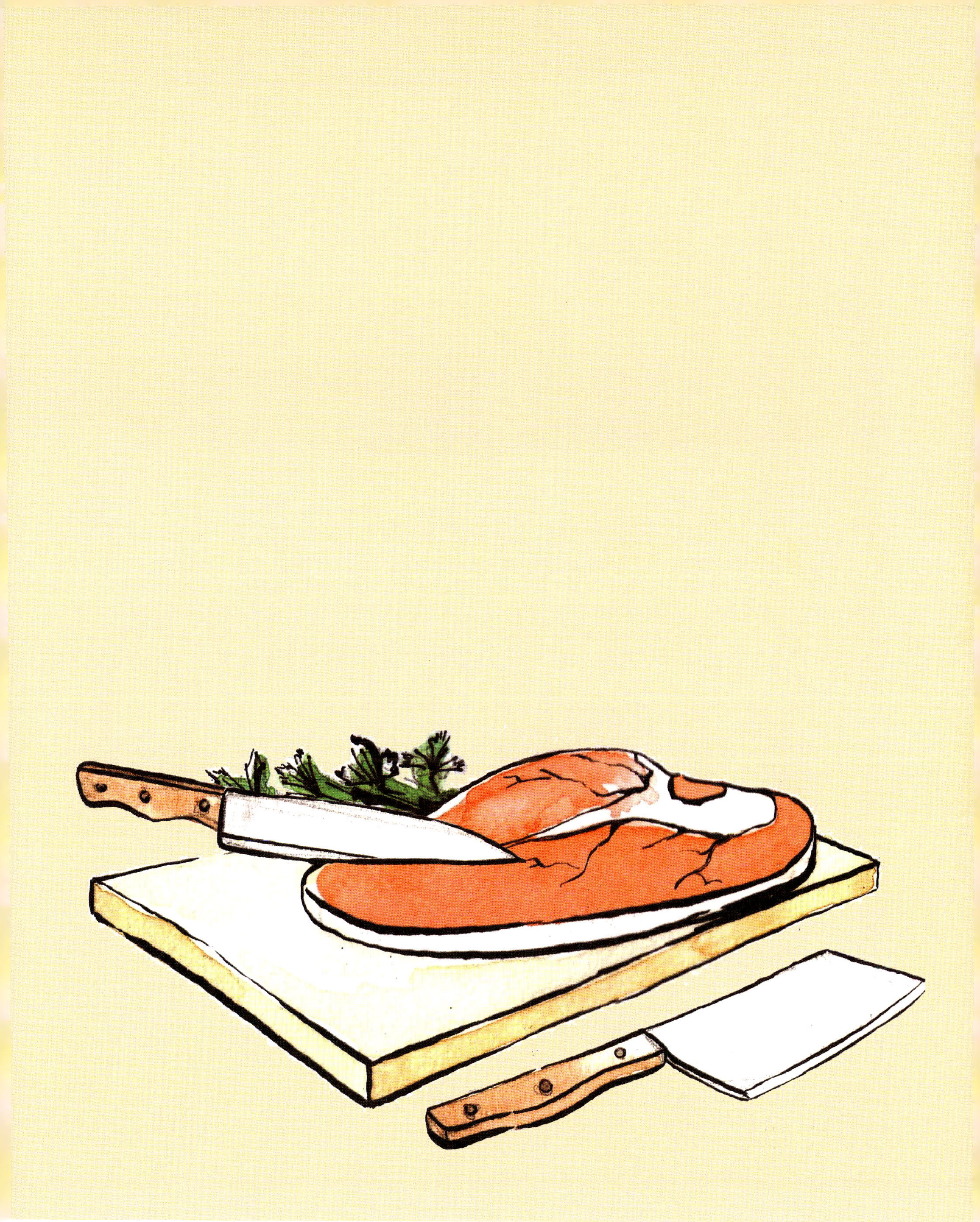

Stuffed Artichokes

Ingredients:
300g minced meat
2 tablespoons oil or ghee
10 pieces artichokes bottom parts (frozen)
2 finely chopped onions
½ a cup tomato paste
Salt and black pepper to season
Cinnamon and sweet pepper to season

Method
1. Cook artichokes in a large saucepan of boiling water until tender then drain.
2. Heat the oil in a pan and cook onions until soft. Add minced meat breaking up any lumps with the back of a wooden spoon. Cook until meat is well browned.
3. Stir in the tomato paste, seasonings and 1 ½ cups of water. Bring to the boil then reduce the heat until the sauce thickens.
4. Line the artichokes in a deep casserole dish. Spoon the mixture in each one and pour the béchamel sauce over the artichokes. Sprinkle cheese on top. Bake in the oven until golden.

Béchamel Sauce

Ingredients:
2 cups milk
40g butter
1 ½ tablespoons plain flour
½ a teaspoon nutmeg
Salt to season

Method:
1. Melt the butter in a medium pan. Add flour and cook, stirring for a minute. Remove from heat.
2. Gradually blend in milk and seasonings stirring over medium heat until the sauce boils and thickens. Remove from heat.

Sheikh Al Meshshi

Ingredients:
600g eggplants
300g minced meat
3 finely chopped onions
½ a cup pine nuts
200g tomato puree
½ a cup water
2 tablespoons ghee or oil
Oil for frying
Salt and cinnamon to season
Black pepper and all spice (sweet pepper) to season

Note: Brush tray with little oil, layer the eggplant.
Brush with oil, bake in the oven until golden.

Method:
1. Peel the eggplants and cut into medium cubes, soak in water for 15 minutes then pat dry on towel. Deep fry until golden then remove from heat drain on kitchen towel.
2. Heat the oil in a pan, cook onions until soft and add minced meat breaking up any lumps with the back of wooden spoon, until meat is browned.
3. Stir in the tomato puree, seasonings and water and bring to the boil. Reduce heat and maintain until sauce thickens.
4. Arrange eggplants in a casserole dish and spread sauce on top. Bake for 30 minutes. Serve with vermicelli rice (Ref. pg 108-109) or plain rice.

Maklouba

Ingredients:
500g eggplants
300g minced meat
3 cups long grain rice
1 diced tomato
1 chopped onion
2 tablespoons ghee
Oil for frying
¼ cup pine nuts
Sprinkle of salt
Sprinkle of cinnamon
Sprinkle of Black Pepper

Note: Use fried cauliflower instead of eggplant.

Method:
1. Peel the eggplants and cut them to medium wedges, soak in water for 15 minutes, pat dry on a towel. Deep fry until golden, remove from heat and drain on a kitchen towel.
2. Boil the rice in a large pan with all the seasonings until cooked. Drain and keep aside.
3. Heat ghee in a pan, cook onion and pine nuts until golden. Add the minced meat breaking any lumps. Sprinkle with salt and add tomatoes. Cook until the meat is cooked.
4. Place a layer of rice in the pan and top with eggplants. Spread the minced meat on top with another layer of rice.
5. Simmer at low heat for 20 minutes. Turn on a serving plate and serve with salad.

Baked Scallops

Ingredients:
1 kg minced meat
2 ½ cups stale breadcrumbs
2 eggs
8 thin slices Gruyere cheese
5 thin slices ham and turkey or chicken
3 tablespoons soft butter
¼ cup water
Salt and black pepper to season
Sprinkle of cinnamon powder

Method:
1. In a large bowl place the minced meat, eggs, seasonings and crumbs. Use your hands to knead well. Add water and mix to obtain a smooth mixture.
2. Grease a shallow dish with butter, place half of the mixture on the dish, using damp hands, and press to smooth the surface.
3. Layer the ham and cheese and cover with the rest of the minced meat. Smooth the surface and slice it to squares greasing the top with butter.
4. Bake until lightly browned. Add water and bake for 5 more minutes.

Dan's Steak

Ingredients:
4 sliced grilled steaks.
1 chopped medium onion
2 cloves crushed garlic
1 tablespoon oil
¼ cup soya sauce
Salt and black pepper to season
1 tablespoon sugar

Method:
1. Heat the oil in a saucepan. Cook the onion and garlic until soft. Add steak with seasonings.
2. Add soya sauce with sugar, stir over low heat until the sauce thickens. Serve with rice or as a sandwich.

Bamya with Meat (okra)

Ingredients:
800g fresh or frozen okra
500g rib steak
6 garlic cloves crushed
4 red tomatoes puree
150g chopped fresh coriander
2 tablespoons ghee or oil
2 ½ cups water or stock
1 ½ teaspoons salt
½ a teaspoon sweet pepper
½ a teaspoon black pepper
1 teaspoon cinnamon
4 tablespoons pomegranate molasses

Method:
1. Cut the rib steak into large cubes. Place the meat in a pan with water and boil until soft. Drain and keep the stock aside.
2. Remove the okra tips, wash well, pat dry and fry until lightly golden.
3. Heat the oil in a large pan, cook garlic and coriander for 3 minutes and add tomato puree, water, molasses and seasonings. Bring to boil.
4. Add okra and meat, simmer at medium heat until okra is tender and the sauce thickens slightly. Serve with rice. (Ref. pg 108)

Mustard Steak

Ingredients:
1 ½ beef eye fillet steak
3 potatoes cut into French fries
4 tablespoons butter
2 tablespoons mustard seeds
300ml fresh cream
5 tablespoons French mustard
Salt and black pepper to season

Method:
1. Heat the butter in a large frying pan. Add steak in a single layer and cook on each side until browned. Place in a dish and keep aside.
2. Add mustard seeds to the same pan and stir for a minute adding in the cream, mustard and seasonings. Boil while stirring constantly until the sauce thickens slightly.
3. Place the potatoes in a shallow ovenproof dish topped with steak. Pour cream mixture on top. Bake until bubbly.

Potato Stew

Ingredients:
700g potatoes
300g of lamb chops or veal
1 tablespoon ghee or 2 tablespoons oil
2 chopped onions
2 tablespoons tomato paste
3 garlic cloves crushed
Water or stock
1 teaspoon salt
½ a teaspoon black pepper
½ a teaspoon sweet pepper
½ a teaspoon cinnamon

Method:
1. Place the lamb in a pan with water; bring to boil, until soft. Drain and keep the stock aside.
2. Heat the oil in a pan and cook the onions until soft. Add the garlic and stir for a minute then stir in the tomato paste, water and seasonings. Simmer over medium heat.
3. Add lamb chops over the sauce, cut the potato to medium cubes, combine with the sauce and simmer until the potato is soft. Remove from heat and serve with rice. (Ref. pg 108)

Steak with Grape juice

Ingredients:
8 small veal steaks
2 grated carrots
½ a cup frozen or fresh peas
1 cup chopped fresh mushroom
1 chopped green capsicum
½ a cup grated mozzarella cheese
2 tablespoons corn oil
1 ½ cups grape juice
1 ½ tablespoons plain flour
Salt and black pepper to season

Method:
1. Heat the oil in a pan and combine all the vegetables. Stir-fry with seasonings until tender then remove from pan.
2. Cover the meat with plastic wrap and pound until thin. Place about 2 tablespoons of the vegetable mixture on each piece of steak. Sprinkle cheese on top.
3. Roll the steaks and add to the same pan of vegetables with 1 tablespoon of oil adding rolls in single layers. Cook until brown and tender then remove from pan.
4. In the same pan mix flour with grape juice. Boil over medium heat stirring until the sauce thickens. Place the meat rolls in a deep serving plate, pour sauce over and serve with mashed potato, salad or steamed vegetables.

Pistachio Roast

Ingredients:
1 kg minced meat
3 egg yolks
2 cups breadcrumbs
1 cup unsalted pistachio
Extra plain flour
4 garlic cloves crushed
2 tablespoons oil
Salt and black pepper to season

Method:
1. Combine minced meat, yolks, garlic, breadcrumbs and seasonings in a large bowl. Mix well.
2. Roll mixture to a long thick stick, flatten slightly with hand, spread pistachio, close and roll tight. Toss in extra flour.
3. Heat oil in a large pan. Add minced meat rolls. Cook in circular motion until browned. Drain on absorbent paper and serve with sauce.

Sauce:
Ingredients:
1 cup red wine (or grape juice)
1 tablespoon white vinegar
1 bay leaf
1 chopped medium onion
3 garlic cloves
1 chopped carrot
½ a cup fresh parsley
2 cups water
1 tablespoon flour

Method:
1. In a large pan place all the ingredients, then boil until they soften.
2. Place in a food processor until smooth and pour it back to pan. Simmer on low heat.
3. Put the minced meat roll to simmer for 5 minutes. Remove and combine with a tablespoon of flour stirring until sauce thickens.
4. Pour sauce over the roll in a deep serving plate. Serve it sliced with sauce on top.

Spinach with Meat

Ingredients:
900g fresh or frozen spinach leaves
500g minced meat
5 cloves crushed garlic
1 tablespoon ghee or 2 tablespoons corn oil or canola oil
½ a cup lemon juice
3 cups water or stock
1 teaspoon salt
½ a teaspoon black pepper
1 teaspoon sweet pepper (all spice)

Hint: Use nut of veal or lamp chops (boiled) instead of mince meat.

Method:
1. In a large bowl soak spinach leaves with water. Clean well and drain (frozen, packets no need to soak in water).
2. Heat the oil in a large pan and cook the garlic until soft. Add the minced meat, breaking any lumps. Combine spinach, seasonings, stock and lemon juice.
3. Boil for 5 minutes. Simmer over low heat until the spinach is tender. Serve with rice.
(Ref. pg 108)

Beef Burger

Ingredients:
500g minced meat
2 finely chopped onions
1 egg
1 cup breadcrumbs
½ a cup tomato puree
Salt and pepper to season

Method:
1. In a large bowl combine all well and shape into thick patties.
2. Heat the oil in a frying pan and cook patties on both sides well cooked.
Heat the buns. Add lettuce, tomatoes, cheese slices, mayonnaise and ketchup.
Serve with French fries

Dan's Burger

Ingredients:
1 kg minced meat
3 medium onions grated
3 cloves crushed garlic
4 finely sliced onions crispy fried
¾ cup breadcrumbs
Salt and black pepper to season

Ingredients:
1. In a large bowl combine all except for crispy onions. Shape into 6 to 8 thick burgers. Heat the oil in a frying pan and cook the patties on both sides until well cooked. You can also grill the patties.
2. Grill the buns. Add lettuce, cheese slices, and crispy onion on top. Serve with salad and ketchup for dipping.

Lubieh Bil Lahm (Green beans with meat)

Ingredients:
800g fresh green beans
500g lamb chops
500g red tomato puree
2 finely chopped onions
8 cups water or stock
2 tablespoons oil
or 1 tablespoon ghee butter
Salt and cinnamon to season
Black pepper and sweet pepper to season

Method:
1. Place the chops in a pan with water and bring to boil until soft. Drain and keep the stock aside.
2. Trim the green beans and remove any strings. Wash under cold water. Drain and cut in length.
3. Heat the oil in a large pan and cook the onions until lightly golden. Add the beans toss with the onions.
4. Combine tomato puree, water and seasonings. Toss well to mix with the beans. Add the meat and simmer over medium heat until the beans are tender and the sauce slightly thickens. Serve with vermicelli rice. (Ref. pg 109)

Dan's Bean Steak

Ingredients:
6 beef eye fillet steaks
2 tablespoons butter
2 thinly sliced carrots
1 finely chopped onion
¼ cup red wine or grape juice
1 large can tomato beans
Salt and black pepper to season

Method:
1. Wrap the steaks with cling film and pound them until thin. Melt the butter in a large frying pan. Add steaks in a single layer and cook on both sides. Remove from pan and slice to strips.
2. Add the onion and carrots. Fry until lightly browned. Add the steaks, seasonings and juice. Bring to boil, reduce heat, cover and simmer for 5 minutes.
3. Combine tomato beans with the mixture and simmer over low heat for 5 minutes. Remove from heat and serve with bread or baked potatoes.

MEATS

Beef Pastry

Ingredients
1kg beef fillet
500g puff pastry
3 medium eggplants
100g mushrooms
50g sundried tomatoes
300g fresh spinach
4 tablespoons olive oil
1 egg yolk
Salt and black pepper to season

Method:
1. Tie the fillets with a string and press the black pepper over the meat. Heat the oil in baking dish. Add the meat and sear on all sides until browned. Bake in the oven for 10 minutes then remove from pan and cool. Reserve the pan drippings for sauce.
2. In a food processor, place the eggplants, mushrooms and sundried tomatoes and process the whole to a paste.
3. Remove the string from the meat and spread the paste over the entire surface. Sprinkle salt on top.
4. Roll out the pastry to a rectangle, spreading some spinach leaves and topping with meat. Place it topside down position and cover it with spinach at center.
5. Fold the two outside edges of the pastry over the meat and seal with the egg yolk. Press the ends together with your fingers and fold under the roll.
6. Brush with egg yolk and fold ends towards the center.
7. Turn the right side up again while brushing with egg yolk. Bake at high temperature for 7 minutes. Reduce to moderate heat and bake for 25 to 30 more minutes. Remove from oven. Cut to slices and serve.

Pan Dripping Sauce:

Ingredients:
2 tablespoons flour
2 cups water
1 beef stock
Salt and black pepper

Method:
Put baking dish with dripping over high heat until dark brown, add flour, stir and remove from heat, add water, beef stock cubes, salt and pepper, simmer for 10 mins, strain and use it over sliced beef.

Shawarma

Ingredients:
750g rump steak
2 sliced onions
2 sliced lemons
¼ cup vinegar
¼ cup oil
¼ cup wine
Salt and black pepper

Method:
1. Slice meat across the grain evenly into long thin strips. Combine onions, lemons, vinegar, oil, wine, salt and pepper. Add meat, stir to coat.
2. Refrigerate the coated meat overnight, covered with plastic wrap. Place in an ovenproof dish, bake in hot oven until well browned. Remove from oven.
3. To serve, spread Tahini mixture in Lebanese bread adding some sliced pickles and topping with meat. Roll the bread folding one end.

Note: Another way for shawarma: Omit wine and lemon slice, place it with 1 cup plain yoghurt. (Ref. pg 262)

Molokhia (Jute Mallow)

Ingredients:
1kg fresh chopped molokhia leaves
500g finely chopped fresh coriander
1 garlic clove crushed
½ a cup lemon juice
2 tablespoons ghee
500g boiled meat chunks
1 whole boiled chicken
5 to 6 cups chicken stock
2 teaspoons salt
½ a teaspoon black pepper
½ a teaspoon sweet pepper
1 teaspoon cinnamon

Method:
1. Wash Molokhia leaves well, drain and dry on a large kitchen towel.
2. Heat the oil in a large pan. Cook the garlic and coriander until soft. Add Molokhia leaves and stir until well coated.
3. Add meat and shredded chicken. Pour the stock to cover while adding the seasonings and lemon juice. Boil for 5 minutes then simmer for 50 more minutes until the leaves are tender. Remove from heat. Serve with plain rice. (Ref. pg 108)

Sauce:

Mix 1 grated onion with 1 cup apple vinegar.

Bread:

Toast slices of Lebanese bread.

How to serve

Place some rice on a serving plate. Top with Mulukhia and spread crushed bread on top, drizzle with vinegar.

Hint:
Might need more water or stock.
Use meat (lamb chops or lamb meat shoulder).
Mix meat and chicken together.

Four Types of Meatball

Type 1

Ingredients:
500g minced meat
4 fresh toast breads (trim the crust)
½ a cup boiled milk
2 tablespoons chopped fresh parsley
2 garlic cloves crushed
1 egg
¼ cup grated cheese, Cheddar-Romano-Parmesan mix
1 mozzarella cheese cut to small cubes
2 cups stale breadcrumbs
1 can chopped tomatoes
2 tablespoons oil
Salt and Black pepper to season

Method:
1. Process bread to fine crumbs.
2. In a small bowl soak bread in milk to soften. Squeeze excess milk and place bread in a big bowl.
3. Combine meat with bread, parsley, garlic, egg, grated cheese and seasonings to a medium sticky mixture.
4. Place 2 tablespoons of mixture in one hand, add one cube of mozzarella cheese, roll to a slightly flat ball and roll in breadcrumbs.
5. Place oil in large frying pan, and fry meatball until golden, drain on paper towel (or bake in the oven).
6. In the same pan, combine tomato, a cup of stock, ground basil salt and pepper. Bring to boil.
7. In an ovenproof deep dish place the meatball, pour sauce over, and bake in a moderate oven for 15 minutes. Serve with pasta, boiled or mashed potato.

Type 2

Ingredients:
500 g minced meat
4 pieces freshly toasted bread (trim the crust)
2 tablespoons fresh chopped parsley
½ a cup grated Parmesan cheese
1 cup flour
2 eggs
Any heavy gravy sauce cooked with red wine of your choice.
2 tablespoons oil
½ a cup boiled water
Salt and white pepper

Method:
1. Process bread to fine crumbs.
2. In a small bowl soak bread in water to soften. Squeeze excess water and place bread in a big bowl.
3. Combine meat with bread, parsley, cheese, eggs, salt and pepper to a medium dough.
4. Roll 3 tablespoons of mixture into balls and roll balls in flour. Heat oil in a large frying pan and cook the meatballs until fried and golden (or bake in the oven).
5. In the same pan add gravy and wine. Simmer for 15 minutes until meat is tender. Serve with mashed potato.

Type 3

Ingredients:
500g minced meat
4 pieces freshly toasted bread (trim the crust)
1 ½ cans chopped tomatoes
½ a kg sliced fresh mushrooms
½ a cup grated Parmesan cheese
Slices mozzarella cheese
1 tablespoon chopped fresh basil
1 tablespoon chopped fresh parsley
2 eggs
¼ cup grounded pine nuts
2 cups stale breadcrumbs
½ a cup boiled milk
2 tablespoons oil
Salt and black pepper

Method:
1. Process bread to fine crumbs
2. In a small bowl soak bread in milk to soften, squeeze excess milk and place bread in a big bowl.
3. Combine meat with bread, basil, parsley, egg, pine nuts, Parmesan cheese, salt and pepper to a medium dough.
4. Roll 3 tablespoons of mixture into balls and roll over breadcrumbs. Heat oil in a large frying pan and fry meatballs until golden. Place them in an ovenproof plate (or bake in the oven).
5. In the same frying pan cook mushrooms until golden, add tomatoes and seasonings. Boil for 5 minutes, pour over meatballs and add sliced mozzarella over each meatball. Bake in the oven for 5 to 10 minutes.

Type 4

Ingredients:
500g minced meat
4 pieces freshly toasted bread (trim the crust)
3 tablespoons pine nuts
3 tablespoons dried raisins
1 egg
½ a cup Parmesan cheese
¼ cup chopped fresh basil
2 finely chopped medium onions
2 cans tomato puree
1 cup cream
¼ cup red wine (optional)
½ a cup boiled milk
1 tablespoon olive oil
Salt and black pepper

Method:
1. Process bread to fine crumbs.
2. In a small bowl soak bread in milk to soften, squeeze excess milk and place bread in a big bowl.
3. Combine meat with bread, pine nuts, raisins, egg, cheese and basil. Season well with salt and pepper.
4. Roll 1 tablespoon of mixture into balls and leave aside. Heat oil in a medium pan, cook onion until lightly golden. Add tomato puree and wine. Boil for 5 minutes. Combine meatballs and cream folding carefully until meat is cooked and sauce thickens. Remove from heat and serve.

Kafta

Ingredients: Basic Kafta
1 kg minced meat
2 cups finely chopped fresh parsley
2 grated onions
Salt and Black pepper
Sweet pepper

Preparation:
Combine all in a bowl mix well and leave aside.

Method 1: Patties
Shape the meat into thick patties, fry or grill. Serve with salad.

Method 2: Arayes
Spread butter or olive oil on Lebanese bread, press some of the Kafta in a thin layer and fold the bread in half. Grill or toast then slice to serve.

Method 3: Tahini
Roll 1 tablespoon of mixture into a ball or sausage shape, grill or fry then dip in Tahini sauce. (ref. pg 117)

Method 4: Dawood Basha
Roll 1 tablespoon of mixture into a ball shape, heat oil in a medium pan fry meat until browned, remove and keep aside. In the same pan, fry 2 tablespoons of pine nuts until golden, add 3 thinly sliced onions until soft add 2 tablespoons of tomato paste, water to cover and seasonings. Boil for 7 minutes, add meat over and simmer for 10 minutes. Serve with rice.

Method 5: Baked
Press Kafta in a rectangular oven tray. Top with 4 sliced fried onions, top with 5 sliced fried potatoes, top with sliced tomato, add 1 cup of water. sprinkle salt. Bake in a moderate oven until the Kafta is cooked. Serve with salad or rice.

Method 6: Tartar
Kafta meat must be very fresh. Press it in a serving plate, drizzle with olive oil and scatter mint leaves on top. Serve with Lebanese bread and garlic dip. (ref. pg 18)

Method 7: Pizza Kafta
Press Kafta into a round baking tray, spread tomato ketchup toped with sliced mushroom, capsicum and black olives. Sprinkle cheese and bake in a hot oven until the meat is cooked. Cut in wedges and serve with salad.

Method 8: With vegetables
Dust your hand with flour and roll 2 tablespoons of Kafta into a sausage shape. Cook in a lightly oiled frying pan until brown. Remove and keep in an ovenproof dish. Add fried zucchini cut into Julienne and fried potato wedges. Combine with Kafta. In a pan, fry chopped onions until golden. Add sliced garlic, tomato puree and seasonings. Boil for 5 minutes then pour over Kafta and bake the whole in hot oven for 10 minutes.

Method 9: Stuffed kafta
Combine 500g of grated mozzarella cheese with 250g of grated cheddar cheese and 500 g well chopped fresh mushrooms. Roll 2 tablespoons of Kafta into a ball shape and press the cheese mixture into the center. Close up the ball form completely.
In a small bowl, whisk egg with dried mint, basil and oregano. Dip the Kafta ball in and roll it on breadcrumbs. Brush the oven tray with olive oil, spread the Kafta and bake in a hot oven while flipping the Kafta until lightly brown.

Tahini Sauce:

Ingredients:
¼ cup Tahini
¼ cup lemon juice
½ a cup water
Sprinkle of salt

Method:
Mix and whisk all the ingredients very well into a smooth light paste. If too thick, add some extra water.

Habra (Raw)

Ingredients:
500g fresh minced lamb meat
1 small grated onion
7 mint leaves
1 teaspoon salt

Hint: Shape to burgers, grill, or fry them

Method:
1. In a food processor place onion, mint and salt. Process until creamy and add the meat. Process all for few seconds.
2. Place meat on a serving plate. Drizzle with olive oil. Serve with Lebanese bread and garlic dip.
(Ref. pg 72-18)

Kibbé Habra (Raw)

Hint: Shape to burgers, grill, or fry them

Ingredients:
500g fresh minced lamb meat
1 small grated onion
3 tablespoons cracked wheat
5 mint leaves
1 tablespoon salt
Sprinkle of pepper

Method:
1. In a small bowl, add boiling water to cracked wheat. Soak for 10 minutes. Drain and squeeze excess water.
2. Place onion, mint, seasonings and cracked wheat in a food processor and process until soft. Combine meat and process for 1 additional minute.
3. Place the product on a serving plate, drizzle with olive oil. Serve with Lebanese bread and garlic dip.
(Ref. pg 72-18)

Freekeh

Ingredients:
1 kg lamb meat shoulder
2 cups cracked grain Freekeh
2 chicken stock cubes
3 cups water
2 tablespoons butter
Salt and pepper to season

Method:
1. In a large pan or pressure cooker, cook lamb shoulder until soft and tender. Remove from pan reserve the stock. Shred the meat.
2. Wash Freekeh well and soak for 10 minutes. Drain and combine with meat, stock and cook until Freekeh is tender.
3. Add butter and seasonings. Simmer over low heat for 10 minutes. Remove from heat and serve hot. It must be medium creamy.

Note: Freekeh is roasted green wheat available in supermarkets.

Whole Roasted Lamb

Ingredients:
5 to 7kg whole lamb
2 tablespoons oil
1 tablespoon saffron threads
Salt to season
2 tablespoons mixed spices
1 cup plain yoghurt

Filling

Ingredients:
5 finely chopped onions
5 boiled eggs
1 cup boiled yellow split peas
½ a cup cashew nuts
½ a cup almonds
½ a cup raisins
1 chopped capsicum
Mixed spices and salt to season

Method:
Combine all, mix well and stuff the lamb before baking.

Method:
1. In a large oven tray, roll an aluminum foil length wise and width
2. Whisk spices, oil, saffron, salt and 4 tablespoons of water and yoghurt. Rub the lamb all over, stuff it with filling, fold the aluminum and bake in hot oven for an hour. Reduce heat and cook for 2 hours more or until well done.

Grilled Meat

Hint: Lamb chops are great with marinating grilled or baked with sauce.

Ingredients:
500g lamb or beef cut into cubes
2 onions cut to four pieces
1 capsicum chopped into cubes
¼ cup olive oil
1/3 cup vinegar
Salt, black and white pepper to season

Method:
1. Whisk all ingredients in a medium bowl. Add meat stirring well to coat. Store in refrigerator covered with plastic wrap overnight. Drain meat and reserve the marinade.
2. Thread meat, onion wedges and capsicum alternately onto oiled skewers. Place them on a grill and cook until tender brushing them with marinade.

Kebabs

Ingredients:
750g minced meat lamb or beef
2 garlic cloves crushed
1 grated onion
1 diced small tomato
Salt, black and sweet pepper to season

Method:
1. Combine minced meat, garlic, onion, tomato and seasoning and mix well.
2. Divide the meat mixture into 12 portions. Mould into sausage shapes around oiled metals skewers.
3. Place skewers on a grill and cook while occasionally turning until cooked. Serve with Hummus or Tahini dip. (Ref. pg 11-117)

Roasted lamb legs

Ingredients:
2 kg lamb legs
10 garlic cloves crushed
Mixed steamed vegetables
Salt and black pepper to season

Gravy:
Ingredients:
2 tablespoons plain flour
2 cups stock
1 tablespoon butter
Salt and pepper to season

Method:
1. Make 10 deep slits in the lamp using a knife. Insert garlic in each slit.
2. Rub the meat with seasonings, place on a roasting rack in a deep baking dish. Roast for about 2 hours. Remove from oven. Serve with gravy and vegetables, or on bed of rice.

Method:
1. Heat pan juice until browned, add flour and stir until lightly golden.
2. Add stock and butter. Stir constantly until gravy boils and thickens.

Ablama

Ingredients:
400g minced meat
600g small sized zucchini
½ a cup pine nuts
1 can tomato puree
3 cups water or stock
Oil for frying
Salt and black pepper to season
Cinnamon and sweet pepper to season

Method:
1. Hollow out the zucchini with a corer, being careful not to pierce the skins.
2. Deep fry the zucchini until the color turns to light gold and drain on absorbent kitchen towel or boil.
3. Heat the oil and add the pine nuts while stirring until light golden. Add the meat and cook. Break any lumps and brown.
4. Fill the zucchini with the meat mixture.
5. Combine the tomato, water, salt and black pepper. Boil the mixture for 5 minutes. Remove from heat.
6. Line the zucchinis in a deep oven dish. Pour the tomato sauce on top. Bake in moderate oven until tender. Serve with vermicelli rice. (Ref. pg 109)

Hashwa

Ingredients:
500g minced meat
2 finely chopped onions
2 tablespoons ghee or oil
¼ cup pine nuts
1 teaspoon nutmeg
1 tablespoon salt
½ a teaspoon black pepper
1 teaspoon cinnamon

Method:
1. Heat the oil in a large frying pan. Cook the onions until golden. Add the pine nuts and stir for two minutes.
2. Stir in the minced meat and seasonings, breaking any lumps until browned.

Note:
1. To be used alone, served with Lebanese bread
2. To be served with scrambled eggs on top
3. To be used as filling for Kibbé.
4. To be used with rice and chicken.
5. To be mixed with rice and served with roasted lamp.

Home Made Sausage

Ingredients:
750g minced beef
250g minced lamb
2 garlic cloves crushed
1 medium sized grated onion
1 egg
50g chopped brie cheese
½ a tablespoon ground dry mint
Salt and black pepper to season

Method:
1. Combine minced beef and lamb in a bowl. Mix the garlic, onion, egg, cheese, mint and seasonings.
2. Using wet hands, mould the mixture to a sausage shape.
3. Place the sausages on a slightly oiled grill or bake in a hot oven. Flip occasionally while cooking. Serve with ketchup, mustard and pickles. (Ref. pg 20-48)

Pepper Steak

Ingredients:
6 thick fillet steaks
2 tablespoons butter
250g fresh cream
2 tablespoons cracked black pepper
Sprinkle of salt

Method:
1. Sprinkle each steak with cracked pepper and press it. Heat butter in frying pan. Add steaks, cook on each side until lightly browned. Remove from pan.
2. Add cream to pan, stir until heated. Sprinkle salt over the steaks. Serve with baked potato and steamed vegetables.

Note: Add sliced mushroom in step two.

Beef with Egg

Ingredients:
600g minced meat
1 cup breadcrumbs
1 egg
5 eggs boiled hard
Salt and black pepper to season

Sauce:

Ingredients:
1 can tomato puree
2 garlic cloves crushed
½ a cup water
Salt and black pepper
Sprinkle of ground dry oregano

Method:
1. Mix well mince meat, breadcrumbs, egg and seasonings in a large bowl.
2. Roll 2 tablespoons of the mixture to a ball, then flatten and place a ½ boiled egg and enclose it completely, re-rolling to an oval shape.
3. Place the meat on a greased oven tray, bake until browned, turning during cooking.
4. Place all the ingredients of the sauce in a medium pan bring to the boil, simmer on low heat until thicken. Serve warm over the meat.

Note: Roll 1 tablespoon of mixture to a ball, then flatten, place an olive and enclose it completely, re-rolling to a ball and as shown in above method.

Stuffed Lamb Ribs

Ingredients:
½ a whole rack of lamb ribs
300g minced meat
½ a cup rice
¼ cup pine nuts
2 tablespoons butter
1 teaspoon salt
½ a teaspoon black pepper
½ a teaspoon cinnamon
½ a teaspoon nutmeg
1 bay leaf

Method:
1. Cut a deep slit between the meat and the bones to create a pocket for the filling.
2. Melt butter, fry pine nuts until golden add minced meat, cook until browned in a frying pan, breaking any lumps.
3. Combine the meat mixture rice seasonings in a bowl. Fill the mixture in the pocket of rack of lamb and secure with tooth picks.
4. Use a pressure cooker for fast cooking, place the rack with water, bay leaf and cinnamon stick. Bring to the boil, remove any scum, close and cook for 1 hour or until done. Remove from heat place it in a deep serving plate with the stock add some mixed vegetables for a nice soup.

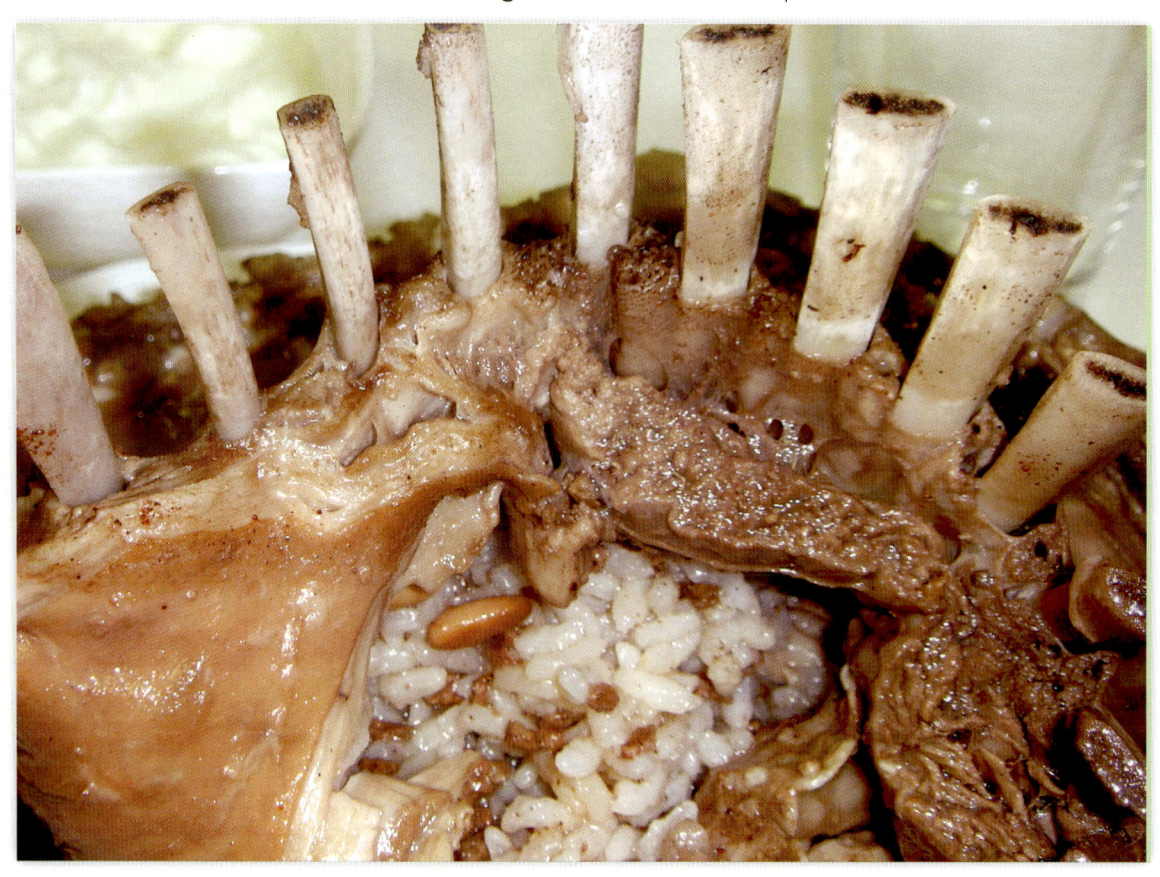

Lamb Cutlets

Ingredients:
12 lamb cutlets
2 tablespoons oil
5 peeled potatoes cut into cubes when baking in the oven.
¼ cup honey
2 tablespoons lemon juice
Salt and black pepper to season

Method:
1. Whisk oil, honey, seasonings and lemon juice well.
2. Combine with cutlets and potato. Toss well, place in an oven-baking tray, bake or grill uncovered turning until browned and tender. Serve with salad.
(Ref. pg 22)

Note: Slice potatoes for grilling.

Lamb Shanks Fatteh

Ingredients:
1 kg cooked lamb shanks (keep stock aside)
3 cups yoghurt
½ a cup Tahini
2 whole toasted Lebanese bread
4 cloves crushed garlic
¼ cup fried pine nuts with butter
¼ cup lemon juice
Sprinkle of salt

Method:
1. Whisk well the yoghurt, garlic, Tahini, lemon juice and salt to a light creamy texture in a large bowl.
2. Break the toasted bread in a deep serving plate. Pour some of the stock just to moist the bread.
3. Remove the meat from bones and spread over bread, top with yoghurt mixture. Sprinkle with pine nuts and the butter. Serve it immediately.

Note: The same method as above, but instead of meat, put Boiled chick peas or fried eggplant; cut into cubes.

Roast Beef Fillet

Ingredients:
1 ½ kg whole beef fillet
3 tablespoons butter
2 cloves crushed garlic
1 tablespoon ground black pepper

Sauce

Ingredients:
1 chopped onion
500g fresh sliced mushrooms
3 cups stock
2 ½ tablespoons plain flour
Salt and black pepper to season

Method:
1. Rub meat all over with the pepper. Melt the butter and garlic in a deep baking dish on top of the stove. Add the meat and brown it all over heat.
2. Place a rack in the dish and put the meat on top, add a cup of water to dish. Bake in the oven until cooked. Cover the meat with pan juice. Remove from heat, leave to rest and slice.
3. Heat the pan juice until browned then remove from heat. Add mushrooms, onion, water, seasonings and flour. Stir on low heat until it bubbles and thickens. Serve over meat slices with baked or mash potato or steamed vegetables.

Note: For extra flavor boil sliced meat with sauce.

Baked Kibbé Dana's

Basic Kibbé:

Ingredients:
500g minced meat
3 cups cracked wheat
1 large grated onion
Cinnamon
1 tablespoon dried marjoram
½ a cup iced water
Salt and black pepper to season
1 tablespoon dried mint

Method:
1. Soak cracked wheat in water for 30 minutes. Drain and squeeze the excess water.
2. Combine the cracked wheat, the meat, the onion and seasonings. Knead well to medium dough.
3. Add small amounts to a food processor and process until smooth paste.
4. Oil a baking dish (32cm*25cm). Divide Kebbé in half using wet hands. Press half of mixture over base of prepared dish; smooth the surface and spread filling over Kebbé layer.
5. Shape the remaining Kebbé into large thin patties. Place over filling to cover the whole, using wet hands to join the patties to be completely covered.
6. Cut through kibbé with wet knife to form diamond shapes. Dot each diamond shape with ghee and drizzle with oil.
7. Bake uncovered in moderate oven for 1 hour until browned. Serve with plain yoghurt or cabbage salad. (Ref. pg 262-28)

Filling (hashwa):

Ingredients:
250g minced meat
2 medium finely chopped onions
½ a cup pine nuts
2 tablespoons oil
Salt and black pepper to season
Cinnamon and Nutmeg

Method:
1. Heat the oil in a frying pan. Stir pine nuts until lightly golden. Add the meat, and break lumps until browned.
2. Stir in onions and seasonings. Cook for 1 minute. Remove from heat.

Kibbé with Laban (Yoghurt)

Ingredients:
Basic kibbé (see page 250)
Filling (see page 250)

Hint: Eat as a snack with salad or cooked in yoghurt

Method:
1. Using wet hands, roll 2 tablespoons of kibbé into a ball. Wet the thumb and press in the middle of the kibbé, turning it around to an oval shape and hollow from inside.
2. Add filling inside the kibbé and close the opening well maintaining the oval shape.
3. Deep fry the kibbé until lightly browned. Drain on absorbent paper.

How to cook the yoghurt

Ingredients:
500g yoghurt
4 cups water
2 tablespoons corn flour
2 garlic cloves crushed
1 tablespoon ground dry mint
Sprinkle of salt

Method:
1. In a large pan, stir water with corn flour. Add yoghurt and salt. Stir on medium heat until it bubbles.
2. Add the kibbé and simmer over low heat for 10 minutes. Remove from heat, stir in garlic and sprinkle mint on top. Serve hot.

Kibbé with Aworma

Ingredients:
Basic kibbé (Ref. pg 250)
Aworma filling or 400g fresh fat minced
¼ cup crushed walnuts
2 finely chopped onions
¼ cup chopped fresh mint leaves
Salt and black pepper to season

Note: We can replace walnuts with pine nuts.

Method:
1. Roll some of the kibbé mixture between 2 nylon wrappers into thin dough.
2. Use a large round cutter and press on the kibbé making 12 circles. Place one tablespoon of filling in 6 of the kibbe circles. Cover with the remaining 6 circles, pressing the edges to form a cup cake.
3. Place them on a baking dish. Bake in hot oven until browned, or grill over barbecue.
4. To freeze them while raw in a single layer on a tray. Place them in freezer bags for up to 3 months.

Aworma

Ingredients:
1 ½ kg minced meat
3 kg minced lamb tail fat
½ a cup salt

Hint:
1. Place 2 tablespoons of awarma in a frying pan and scramble egg with it.
2. Use awarma in Kishik soup.
3. For filling Kebbeh with awarma.

Method:
1. In a large pan cook the minced fat until golden and smaller in size.
2. In a large frying pan combine minced meat with salt and cook breaking any lumps until water evaporates.
3. Combine minced meat with fat, cook stirring occasionally for 15 minutes. Remove from heat.
4. Leave it to cool completely. Place in a container in the fridge. Expires in 7 months.

Cham's Chili Con Carne

Ingredients:
500g minced meat
5 finely chopped onions
10 garlic cloves crushed
400g canned red kidney beans
2 tablespoons tomato paste
1 chicken stock cube
2 cups water
1 tablespoon oil
1 tablespoon sugar
Sprinkle of chili powder
Salt and black pepper to season

Method:
1. Heat the oil in a large pan. Add onion and garlic and stir until light golden. Add minced meat. Cook until well browned breaking any lumps.
2. Add beans, sugar, salt, pepper, chili, stock, tomato paste and water. Stir well. Simmer for 30 minutes until almost dry.
3. Cut long bread sticks into 1 cm, brush with crushed garlic and butter. Grill in the oven until light golden. Remove from oven.
4. Place bread on a serving plate. Top with meat mixture and drizzle with hot chilli sauce for extra kick.

Laban Emou

Ingredients:
500g boned leg lamb
3 garlic cloves crushed
10 whole baby onions
1 tablespoon ground dried mint.
2 tablespoons corn flour
500g yoghurt
4 cups water
Sprinkle of salt

Method:
1. Cut the meat into 3 cm cubes and boil until cooked.
2. In a large pan stir water or stock with onions, corn flour. Add yoghurt and salt, cook on medium heat stirring until it bubbles.
3. Add meat and simmer over low heat for 10 minutes. Stir in garlic and sprinkle with mint. Serve with rice.

Veal With Cheese

Ingredients:
8 veal steaks
8 slices cheddar cheese
4 tablespoons butter
Salt and black pepper to season

Method:
1. Lightly pound steaks. Melt butter in a large frying pan. Sprinkle steaks with salt and pepper and fry on each side until browned.
2. Remove from pan and drain pan juice and set aside. Put the steaks in an oven dish top each with cheese and put under grill until the cheese just melted. Remove from grill.
3. Add the pan juice, salt and pepper with 1 tablespoon of flour. Stir until lightly thick and remove from heat.
4. Serve steaks with gravy and vegetables.

Hareese

Ingredients:
1 ½ kg boned leg lamp
1 ½ cups pearl barley
4 whole cardamom seeds
2 tablespoons butter
Sprinkle of salt

Method:
1. For fast cooking, use a pressure cooker. Put the meat with water boiling over high heat and remove any scum. Add cardamom. Close the lid and cook on medium heat for 1 hour until meat is very tender.
2. Combine pearl barley with meat. Close the lid and cook for 1 hour. Remove from heat and leave it to cool.
3. Open the lid and add salt to taste. Place all of the mixture in a food processor and process to a creamy texture.
4. Spread in the serving plate and drizzle with melted butter. Serve immediately.

Hint: Sprinkle ground cinnamon.

Shish Barak

Dough:

Ingredients:
2 cups plain flour
3 tablespoons oil
Water
Sprinkle of salt

Method:
1. Combine all to form a dough. Knead dough until smooth and elastic. Cover dough with a cloth and let it stand for 10 minutes.
2. Roll dough on lightly floured board as thin as possible. Cut into rounds using a 5 cm round cutter.
3. Place ½ a teaspoon of filling in the center of each dough, fold round in half and press the edges firmly. Shape dough into cylinders using fore finger and press ends together firmly.
4. Place in an oven tray. Bake until lightly golden then remove from oven. In a large pan, cook yoghurt until it bubbles. Add shish barak and simmer over low heat for 20 minutes, stirring occasionally. Serve alone or with rice.

Filling:
Hashwa or Kafta (Ref. pg 242-233)

Ingredients:
500g yoghurt
4 cups water
2 tablespoons corn flour
Salt to season

Method:
Combine water and corn flour. Mix well adding yoghurt and salt. Simmer over medium heat stirring until yoghurt bubbles.

Mougrabia

Ingredients:
500g dry Mougrabia
5 large lamb shanks
500g peeled baby onions (whole)
1 can chickpeas
3 tablespoons ghee
1 tablespoon butter
1 tablespoon extra caraway powder
1 ½ tablespoon cardamom powder
2 tablespoons caraway powder
½ a tablespoon mixed spices
2 teaspoons salt

Method:
1. Heat oil in a large pan. Cook onion until lightly golden. Remove from oil and keep in a plate.
2. In the same pan, fry the meat, add water to cover and boil until soft. Stir in chickpeas, onions, mixed spices, salt, cardamom and caraway. Simmer over medium heat for 20 minutes.
3. In a large pan bring chicken stock cubes with water to boil. Add mougrabia and cook stirring occasionally until soft. Drain and place it back in the pan. Sprinkle some salt.
4. Heat butter in a small frying pan. Stir in extra caraway until it bubbles. Combine with mougrabia.
5. In a serving plate, spoon mougrabia topped with meat mixture and sauce. Drizzle with vinegar and serve hot.

Dairy Products

Dairy products are the animals gift to us, if we just think how much dairy products enrich our bodies, we'd bow down to them, if it was for the calcium they provide for our bones or the whipped cream on top of our treats. Adding this white magic to any food would be the ultimate upgrade.

Laban (Yoghurt)

Ingredients:
1 kg fresh milk
1 cup plain yoghurt

Method:
1. Boil the milk. Remove from heat, cool and pour in a deep plastic container.
2. Mix in yoghurt. Cover with the lid and wrap the container with a blanket overnight.
3. Next day keep in refrigerator for 5 hours until firm and cool.

Labneh

Ingredients:
1 kg plain yoghurt
2 tablespoons salt

Method:
1. Mix yoghurt and salt in a bowl. Pour in a muslin bag and tie as tightly as possible, leaving a loop at the end.
2. Hang the muslin bag over a bowl to drain for 2 days.
3. Roll a tablespoon of drained yoghurt into balls. Place them on a kitchen towel. Refrigerate for 2 days, changing the towel.
4. Place Labneh in a large jar. Cover with olive oil and keep for 2 weeks in the refrigerator.

Hint: Spread Labneh on a plate, drizzle with olive oil. Serve with olives and bread.

Arisha

Method:
1. Add the reserved whey from the yoghurt in a large pan to boil.
2. While boiling add 4 cups of milk. Stir the milk until it curds. Remove from heat and cool aside.
3. Remove the curds with a slotted spoon. Keep in a plastic container. Refrigerate for 3 to 4 days.
4. Serve with drizzled honey or a sprinkle of sugar.

Note: Whey is the liquid that is drained from the yoghurt

Shanklish (Dry Cheese)

Ingredients:
1 kg plain yoghurt
1 finely sliced tomato
1 finely chopped onion
Fresh parsley
2 tablespoons salt
½ a teaspoon ground chili
Or ½ a teaspoon sweet paprika
½ a cup dry ground oregano

Method:
1. Boil yoghurt in a medium pan. Remove from heat and pour into a muslin bag. Tie the bag tightly. Hang over a bowl to drain for 4 hours.
2. Untie the muslin and stir in salt, paprika then knead it well. Tie the muslin bag and hang till next day.
3. Place oregano on a large plate. Untie the muslin. Roll 3 tablespoons of Shanklish, squeezing and pressing it well to a medium ball.
4. Roll over oregano to coat well. Spread a towel on tray and keep the cheese balls to dry for 3 days before using (turning occasionally).
5. Roughly chop Shanklish. Add finely chopped tomatoes, onion and fresh parsley mix with olive oil. Place it on the plate. Serve with Lebanese bread.

Simple Cheese

Ingredients:
1 ½ kg fresh milk
1 cup plain yoghurt
3 cups yoghurt whey
1 tablespoon sea salt

Method:
1. Boil the milk in a large pan. Stir the yoghurt and whey. Boil for 5 minutes.
2. Line a flat strainer with a large piece of muslin. Spoon the cheese curd and fold muslin to cover. Place a large pan filled with water on top to squeeze. Firm the cheese for 1 hour.
3. In a large container add the liquid from pan; mix with sea salt well.
4. Unite muslin cut cheese to small squares and place them in the whey mixed with salt. Refrigerate. Keep for 2 weeks.

Shami Cheese

Ingredients:
2 cups yoghurt
1 teaspoon lemon

Method:
1. Boil yoghurt in a medium pan until it turns to a curd, almost like cottage cheese. Add lemon juice.
2. Remove from heat. Cool. Squeeze curd and place it on a plate and sprinkle with melted butter. Serve immediately.

Baladi Cheese

Ingredients:
2 kg fresh milk
¼ teaspoon rennet powder
or ½ a rennet tablets

Method:
1. Boil the milk in a large pan. Remove from heat. Slightly stir it to cool.
2. Dissolve rennet in a ¼ glass of tap water. Stir in ½ a teaspoon of salt. Mix well.
3. Combine rennet with milk. Stir for 3 minutes. Pour in a container.
4. Wrap it well with a towel for 3 hours or until firm.
5. Use a large spoon. Break the curd and reserve whey in a container.
6. Add 1 cup of curd. Squeeze well to remove excess water and place on a tray.
7. Make a small hole in center of each cheese with the back of wooden spoon. Add in sea salt and leave on the tray for 1 hour.
8. Place the cheese in the container. Cover with whey. Refrigerate to cool.

Zikra Cheese

Ingredients:
1 zikra cheese
(to use starting step 6
from baladi cheese recipe)

Method:
1. Place the cheese on a kitchen towel for 5 days.
2. Use quantity of Arisha mix with cheese. Place them in a large jar adding Arisha in the cheese to fill any gaps.
3. Close tightly for 24 hours then turn the jar upside down for 4 days.
4. Serve with Lebanese bread or saj, black olives and sliced tomatoes.

Quick Kishik (Green Kishik)

Ingredients:
½ a cup fine cracked wheat (burghul)
1 finely chopped onion
2 tablespoons chopped fresh parsley
½ a kg fresh Labneh (Ref. pg 263)
1 cup boiling water
½ a cup roughly cracked walnut
5 leaves fresh mint
5 black olives
Drizzle of olive oil
Sprinkle of sweet paprika

Method:
1. Soak burghul in the boiling water for 2 hours. Place in a food processor. Process to a soft paste.
2. Combine burghul paste, Labneh, a sprinkle of salt, onion and walnut in a medium bowl.
3. Spoon in a serving plate. Smooth the surface top with olives and mint. Sprinkle with paprika and olive oil.
4. Serve with Lebanese bread.

Green Kishik

Ingredients:
500g white cracked wheat (burghul)
500g plain yoghurt (Laban)
1 ½ kg fresh Labneh
Salt to season

Method:
1. Soak burghul with yoghurt in a large bowl. Leave overnight.
2. Place soaked burghul in batches in a food processor. Process to a fine powder.
3. In a bowl, combine burghul, salt and 1 kg of Labneh and mix to dough. Cover with plastic wrap. Leave overnight.
4. Add ½ a kg of Labneh. Mix well and cover with plastic cover for 4 hours.
5. Roll 2 teaspoons of kishik into a ball. Place them on a towel till the next day.
6. Put kishik in a large jar. Cover with olive oil. Refrigerate for 2 months.

Dry Kishik

Method:
1. Apply the first 4 steps used for green kishik.
2. Spread a large muslin on a table. Sprinkle with flour.
3. Place 1 tablespoon of kishik apart on muslin. Leave to dry well.
4. Put the mix in a large bowl and break them to crumbs. Use a food processor to process batches to a fine powder
5. Spread kishik powder on muslin again. Cover them to dry well.
6. Put the kishik in a bag. Close tightly and refrigerate. Keeps well for one year, use for Kishik soup.

Sweets

Sweets are everybody's sweetheart, it's the little kids' reward, the birthday celebration, wedding commitment, break-ups therapists, and if for no reason at all just for it's euphoric taste that makes us sacrifice our allure for a few sinful bites.

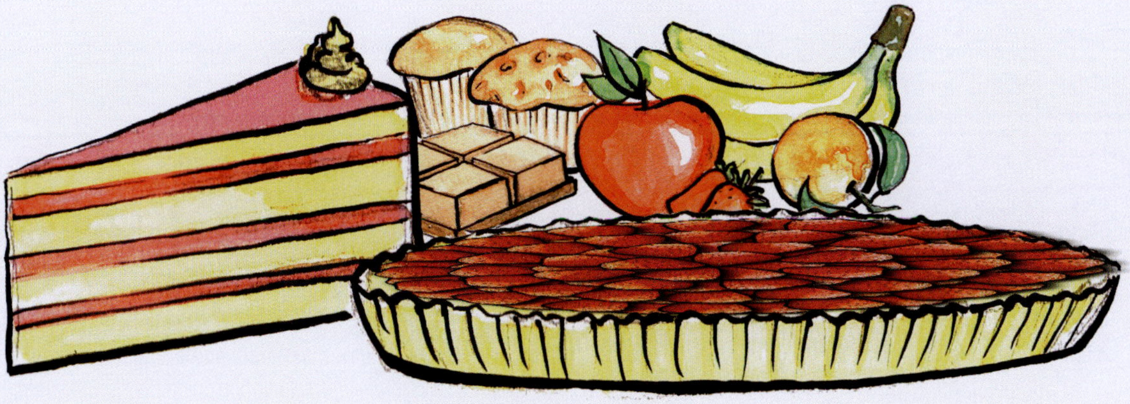

Oats Biscuits

Ingredients:
2 cups plain flour
1 ½ cups sugar
2 cups oats
250g unsalted soft butter
½ a cup golden syrup
1 teaspoon bicarbonate soda
2 tablespoons water

Method:
1. Combine all dry ingredients in a bowl. Mix well.
2. Stir butter syrup in a small pan until butter melts. Remove from heat.
3. Dissolve soda in water. Add to butter mixture.
4. Place butter mixture over the flour until well combined.
5. Roll a tablespoon of dough, flatted slightly on prepared tray.
6. Bake for 15 to 20 minutes.
7. Remove from heat and cool aside.

Ginger Biscuits

Ingredients:
2 cups plain flour
1 cup sugar
125g unsalted butter
¼ cup water
1 tablespoon golden syrup
1 tablespoon ground ginger
½ a teaspoon bicarbonate soda

Method:
1. Combine all ingredients in a bowl. Knead to soft dough.
2. Roll a tablespoon of mixture into balls. Flatten slightly on prepared trays.
3. Bake for 15 to 20 minutes. Remove from heat and leave to cool.

Hibz Rice Bubbles

Ingredients:
5 cups rice bubbles
300g white marshmallows
¼ cup unsalted butter

Method:
1. Place marshmallows and butter in a medium pan. Stir over heat until melted.
2. Stir in rice bubbles. Mix well.
3. Grease lamington pan and press the mixture in. Leave to cool.
4. Slice to medium squares and serve

Gouraiba

Ingredients:
2 cups plain flour
1 cup icing sugar
¼ teaspoon baking powder
¾ to 1 cup ghee
¼ cup pine nut

Method:
1. Beat ghee and sugar in a small bowl until smooth.
2. Stir in flour and baking powder. Knead well.
3. Roll ½ a tablespoon of mixture into balls. Flatten slightly between on your palm. Place on tray and press pine nut seed in the middle.
4. Bake in moderate hot oven for about 10 minutes. Stand for 3 minutes before lifting. Transfer to wire rack.

Rock Biscuits

Ingredients:
2 cups plain flour
1 cup sugar
1 cup ghee
3 beaten eggs
2 teaspoons baking powder
½ a teaspoon nutmeg
½ a cup raisins
½ a cup crushed walnuts
Sprinkle of salt
1 teaspoon cinnamon

Method:
1. Place flour, sugar, salt, baking powder, spices, raisins and walnuts in a large mixing bowl. Stir to combine.
2. Add ghee, using a spoon. Stir until combined. Add eggs and mix well.
3. Drop a tablespoon of mixture into prepared trays. Bake for 10 to 15 minutes until lightly golden. Transfer to wire racks to cool.

Dirzi Biscuits

Ingredients:
2 cups plain flour
1 cup fine semolina
1 ½ cup milk
1 ¼ cup sugar
½ a cup ghee
½ a tablespoon Daat kake
½ a teaspoon ground cinnamon
1 tablespoon ground anise
1 tablespoon baking powder
1 teaspoon yeast

Method:
1. Place flour, semolina, sugar, spices, baking powder and yeast in large mixing bowl. Stir to combine.
2. Add ghee. Using your hands, knead until combined. Add milk gradually. Knead to smooth dough and cover to double in size.
3. Roll a tablespoon of mixture into balls. Place on prepared trays and flatten with a fork in a crisscross pattern.
4. Bake for 20 minutes. Cool on a tray and transfer to wire racks.

Note:
Daat kake:
½ a cup of anise seeds
½ a cup of fennel seeds
½ a cup of nutmeg seeds
1 tablespoon of mahaled grains
½ a teaspoon of Arabic gum

Process all ingredients to fine powder. Place in clean jar.

Kaake Zahle

Ingredients:
5 cups plain flour
1 ¼ cup sugar
2 ½ cups milk
117g unsalted butter
2 tablespoons instant yeast
1 teaspoon ground mahaleb
1 teaspoon fresh ground nutmeg

Method:
1. Combine yeast, milk and butter. Mix well. Add sugar, spices and flour gradually. Knead to soft slightly sticky dough. Cover to double in size.
2. Roll 3 teaspoons of dough into balls. Continue rolling into 5cm length. Carefully fold in half into a ring. Place on a prepared tray. Cover to double in size.
3. Bake in hot oven until golden. Place on wire rack to cool.

Note: A nice breakfast snack.

Anise Biscuits

Ingredients:
2 ½ cups plain flour
½ a cup oil
½ a cup ghee
½ a cup sesame seeds
¼ cup anise seeds
¾ cup sugar
1 teaspoon baking powder

Method:
1. Process all ingredients in a food processor to soft dough.
2. Roll in a tablespoon to a length of 5 cm. Fold in half into a ring. Place on prepared trays.
3. Bake in hot oven until golden. Stand 3 minutes before lifting. Transfer to wire rack to cool.

Sugar Biscuits

Ingredients:
1 ¼ cup plain flour
125g unsalted butter
1 tablespoon baking powder
2 tablespoons Daat Kake
1 cup icing sugar

Method:
1. Combine all ingredients in a medium bowl until smooth.
2. Roll a tablespoon of mixture into balls. Place apart on oven trays. Flatten slightly with a fork.
3. Bake in moderately hot oven for about 10 minutes. Stand 5 minutes before lifting. Place on wire rack to cool.
4. Serve dusted with icing sugar.

Date Rolls

Ingredients:
500g seeded soft dates
1/3 cup unsalted butter
2 cups rice bubbles
Coconut powder

Method:
Combine dates, butter rice bubbles. Knead to soft dough. Roll 1 teaspoon to a ball and roll over the coconut powder to cover and serve.

Date Baklawa

Ingredients:
3 packets plain biscuits
227g unsalted butter
1 kg dates seeded
6 eggs
5 cups sugar
3 cups shredded coconut

Method:
1. Combine dates and melted butter. Knead well. Add sugar, egg and coconut. Place the mixture in a pan on low heat. Stir until combined.
2. Crush biscuits and stir with mixture to a smooth dough. Sprinkle extra coconut on the mixture. Press the mixture over base. Refrigerate for 1 hour.
3. Slice and serve with extra coconut.

Butter Biscuits

Ingredients:
500g butter
2 cups sugar
4 eggs
1 teaspoon vanilla
2 teaspoons baking powder
6 to 7 cups flour

Method:
1. Using electric beaters, beat sugar, eggs, vanilla and butter until light and creamy.
2. Add sifted flour and baking powder and mix to soft dough.
3. Turn out into lightly floured surface and knead until smooth. Roll out to 7 mm thick. Cut out to shapes.
4. Place biscuit on prepared trays. Bake for 15 to 20 minutes in a hot oven or until golden.
5. Place on a wire rack to cool.

Pine Nut Biscuits

Ingredients:
6 cups flour
454g unsalted butter
3 eggs
1 ¼ cup sugar
1 teaspoon vanilla
1 teaspoon lemon zest
2 teaspoons baking powder

Method:
1. Sift flour, baking powder in a large mixing bowl. Add sugar and zest. Mix well.
2. Beat with a mixer butter, eggs, sugar and vanilla to a creamy mixture.
3. Add butter mixture to flour. Stir well until combined. Roll heaped teaspoon of the mixture into balls. Press lightly on extra sugar pressing pine nut in the middle.
4. Arrange on trays with room for spreading. Bake for 10-15 minutes until golden. Cool cookies on tray.

Milk Biscuits

Ingredients:
4 cups plain flour
3 tablespoons heaped milk powder
½ a cup ghee
1 ½ cup sugar
1 cup liquid anise
Sprinkle of ground Mahaleb
Sprinkle of ground nutmeg
Sprinkle of instant yeast

Method:
1. Sift flour, milk powder, Mahaleb, nutmeg and yeast in to large mixing bowl.
2. Combine ghee and sugar anise in small pan. Stir over low heat until ghee melts. Leave till it cools.
3. Add ghee mixture to dry ingredients and knead to smooth dough. Leave aside for 2 hours.
4. Roll the dough and cut circle with cookie cutter and bake until golden (about 10 mins) in hot oven.

Jam Biscuits

Ingredients:
3 cups plain flour
277g unsalted butter
1 ¼ cup icing sugar
½ a teaspoon vanilla
2 egg yolks
Apricot jam or strawberry

Method:
1. Using a food processor, process flour, butter, sugar, yolks and vanilla well to smooth firm dough.
2. Turn out onto lightly floured surface. Roll out to 3 cm. Cut to medium rounds using a fluted cutter.
3. Roll dough again and cut 18 circles using a fluted cutter. Cut out the center of these circles.
4. Bake in moderate oven until golden. Cool.
5. Spread the whole circle with jam and top it with the cutout biscuits, pressing gently to seal.
Sift extra icing sugar over.

Date Fingers

Ingredients:
6 ½ cups plain flour
454g unsalted butter
8 tablespoons icing sugar
8 tablespoons milk powder
½ a tablespoon ground Mahaleb
½ a cup flower water
½ a cup rose water
2 teaspoons baking powder

Method:
1. Using a food processor, process all ingredients to soft dough. Place it in a bowl to rest for 20 minutes.
2. Using your hands, flatten 1 teaspoon of dough. Lay one date finger in the middle and press to seal in a finger shape.
3. Bake in hot oven until golden for 15 to 20 minutes. Place on a wire rack to cool.

Filling:

Ingredients:
900g seeded soft date
¼ cup ghee
1 tablespoon ground nutmeg

Method:
Combine all and knead well. Roll 1 teaspoon into medium fat finger.

Semolina Maammoul

Ingredients:
6 cups plain flour
3 cups fine semolina
9 tablespoons milk powder
9 tablespoons icing sugar
1 ½ tablespoon ground Mahaleb
2 tablespoons baking powder
400g unsalted butter
1 cup oil
½ a cup flower water
½ a cup rose water

Fillings:

Walnut:
500g crushed walnut
¼ cup sugar
4 tablespoons rose water

Combine all well to a soft filling

Pistachio:
500g crushed pistachios
¼ cup sugar
4 tablespoons flower water

Combine all well to a soft filling.

Dates:
500g soft dates
1 tablespoon nutmeg
2 tablespoons ghee

Knead to smooth dough. Roll 1 teaspoon into balls and leave aside.

Method:
1. Combine flour, semolina, milk, sugar, mahaleb and baking powder well in a bowl. Add butter and knead well followed by the oil.
2. Add flower water and rose water. Knead to soft dough. Cover to rest for 2 hours and knead again.
3. Roll 1 tablespoon of dough. Open flat place filling in the middle. Seal well. Press in the mold to have the pattern.
4. Bake in moderate hot oven until lightly golden. Cool and dust with extra icing sugar.

Note: There is a special wooden mould for maamoul. You can find them in stores.
Place the mould in a new clean stocking for easier work.

Mini Apricot Slices

Ingredients:
120g unsalted butter
¾ cup sugar
3 eggs
3 teaspoons baking powder
1 teaspoon vanilla essence
3 cups plain flour
½ a cup apricot jam

Method:
1. Using electric beater, beat butter and sugar until light and creamy. Add eggs, vanilla. Beat well.
2. Combine flour, baking powder and mix to a soft dough.
3. Place two-third of dough in a shallow rectangular tin. Press and smooth the surface with the back of a metal spoon.
4. Spoon jam evenly over dough, coarsely grate reserved dough and sprinkle evenly over the jam.
5. Bake for 30 minutes until golden. Cool in tin. Slice in to squares.

Sweet Macaroon

Ingredients:
2 cups fine semolina
2 cups plain flour
¾ cup oil
1 cup sugar
2 teaspoons baking powder
1 cup water
3 tablespoons ground anise

Method:
1. Combine in a large bowl, semolina, flour, sugar, baking powder, anise and oil.
2. Add water. Knead to medium soft dough. Cover to rest for 30 minutes. Knead again.
3. Divide dough into 4. Roll each batch in to long sausage. Cut in to 2 pieces roll each piece, pressing along the outside of a sieve to give a pattern.
4. Heat oil in a pan and deep fry in batches until golden. Remove from oil and stir in syrup for 1 minute. Remove and place on a serving plate.

Syrup:

Ingredients:
3 cups sugar
1 ½ cup water
1 tablespoon lemon juice
1 tablespoon flower water

Method:
Boil sugar, water very well. Add lemon juice
Boil to mild thick syrup. Stir in flower. Leave it to cool

Dans' Chip Biscuits

Ingredients:
227g unsalted butter
2 cups plain flour
2 eggs
2 ½ cups oatmeal
2 cups sugar
½ a teaspoon cocoa
1 teaspoon vanilla essence
½ a teaspoon salt
1 teaspoon bicarbonate soda
1 teaspoon baking powder
1 ½ macadamia or pecan nuts
24 oz chocolate chip

Method:
1. Using electric beater to mix the butter and sugar until creamy. Add eggs, vanilla essence and beat until the whole combines.
2. Place oatmeal in a food processor. Process to a fine powder. Add over all the dry ingredients in a large bowl. Stir until just combined.
3. Add chocolate chip and nuts and mix well. Roll 1 tablespoon of mixture. Arrange on tray. Allow some room for spreading.
4. Bake for 15 minutes until lightly browned. Leave on tray for 3 minutes. Cool on wire rack.

Ashtah

Ingredients:
5 fresh sliced breads
2 ½ cups milk
1 tablespoon flour
1 tablespoon sugar

Method:
1. Remove crust from bread. Combine with sugar, flour and milk in a medium pan.
2. Stir over heat frequently to a medium thick cream. Boil for an extra minute.
3. Pour in a bowl. Cover with plastic wrap and refrigerate. Stir occasionally. Cool.
4. Put Ashtah in small serving plates. Sprinkle some crushed pistachio and drizzle with honey or syrup.

Cocoa Spread

Ingredients:
227g unsalted butter
4 eggs
1 tablespoon lemon zest
1 teaspoon vanilla essence
4 tablespoons cocoa
7 tablespoons milk powder
7 tablespoons icing sugar

Method:
1. Using a mixer beat eggs, vanilla, lemon zest well. Add sugar, milk and cocoa. Mix well.
2. Add butter and mix well. Pour into clean jars. Refrigerate to firm. Spread mixture on bread.

Aish al Saraya

Ingredients:
16 slices bread
2 cups boiling water
1 ½ cups sugar
¼ cup flower water
1 tablespoon vanilla essence
Crushed pistachio
2 ½ cups Ashta (Ref. pg 288)

Method:
1. Add 1 ½ tablespoons of sugar in a medium pan. Leave on heat to caramelize. Add water. Boil for 2 minutes.
2. Add sugar. Stir to dissolve and remove from heat. Add flower water and vanilla.
3. Combine bread and sauce in a bowl. Stir well. Refrigerate to cool.
4. Pour mixture in a medium serving plate. Spread evenly. Top with 2 ½ cups of Ashta. Spread evenly. Sprinkle pistachio on top.
5. Serve it sliced drizzled with syrup or honey.

Note: Flower water = blossom water.

Coffee Pudding

Ingredients:
3 packets plain biscuits
1 cup instant coffee
1 big can condensed milk
2 cups thick whipped cream
1 cup sugar
½ a cup flaked toasted almonds

Method:
1. In a small pan, stir sugar until golden brown. Add almonds and mix well. Pour on a greased tray. Cool, break to pieces. Crush with a dough roller.
2. Combine whipped cream and condense milk. Fold slowly.
3. Dip biscuits in coffee layers in a deep serving plate. Spoon cream mixture followed by dipped biscuits with a last layer of cream. Refrigerate for 3 hours. Serve sprinkled with crushed sugar.

Moughly

Ingredients:
1 cup rice flour
1 cup sugar
8 cups water
2 tablespoons ground anise
1 tablespoon ground cinnamon
2 tablespoons ground caraway
1 cup flaked almonds
1 cup raisins
1 cup shredded coconut
1 cup whole pistachios
1 cup whole walnuts

Method:
1. Combine rice, sugar and spices in a large pan add water. Stirring frequently on heat until thick and bubbling for 10 minutes.
2. Pour into small serving bowl. Refrigerate to cool. Serve with some almonds, raisins, pistachios and sprinkled walnuts with coconut.

Note: Soak almonds, pistachio and walnuts in water for 5 hours. Peel off the skin.

Jell-o Pudding

Ingredients:
510g thick cream
2 packets strawberry Jell-o
1 cup boiling water
7 tablespoons icing sugar
4 sliced bananas
200g plain biscuits

Method:
1. Combine cream, Jell-o, water, sugar. Add bananas and crushed biscuits. Stir well.
3. Pour in the mold.
3. Refrigerate to harden. Turn on a serving plate and slice to serve.

Note: Add 1 extra cup of water. Mix well. Keep in freezer for some nice strawberry ice cream.

Mehalabia

Ingredients:
3 cups milk
3 tablespoons corn flour
6 tablespoons sugar
2 tablespoons flower water

Method:
1. Stir all ingredients in a medium pan over heat until thick and bubbly. Add flower water. Remove from heat.
2. Pour into small serving bowl. Refrigerate and serve cold.

Mango Pudding

Ingredients:
4 large ripe mangoes
1 big packet Mango Jell-o
1 big packet apricot
5 cups water

Method:
1. Use a food processor to process mango until smooth. Stir Jell-o and water in a bowl. Add mango and stir well. Pour into medium bowl cover with plastic wrap. Refrigerate until firm.
2. Turn on a serving plate. Slice to serve.

Rice Flour Pudding

Ingredients:
2 cups milk
2 tablespoons rice flour
4 tablespoons sugar
1 tablespoon rose water
1/8 teaspoon Arabic gum (mistak gum)

Method:
1. Combine milk, ground rice and sugar in a medium pan on moderate heat. Stirring frequently until thick and bubbly.
2. Remove from heat. Stir rose water and crushed Arabic gum with little sugar.
3. Pour in a small serving bowl. Refrigerate and serve cold.

Cocoa Rice

Ingredients:
1 cup short grain rice
3 tablespoons drinking cocoa
4 tablespoons sugar
1 can sweet condensed milk

Method:
1. Boil the rice in a medium pan until soft. Drain and put it back on low heat.
2. Combine with cocoa and sugar. Stir well.
3. Drizzle condensed milk on top and serve cold or hot.

Semolina Halwahh

Ingredients:
3 cups fine semolina
3 cups sugar
2 cups water
¾ cup ghee
¾ cup pine nuts
1 tablespoon flower water

Method:
1. Heat ghee in a medium pan. Fry pine nuts until golden. Remove and drain on a kitchen towel.
2. Add semolina stir well with sugar, water and flower water until thick.
3. Pour in a small serving bowl. Sprinkle pine nut. Serve cold.

Note: Roll 1 tablespoon of mixture to a ball. Press some pine nut on top and serve.

Ashtalya

Ingredients:
5 cups milk
7 tablespoons corn flour
Sprinkle of sugar
¼ teaspoon Arabic gum
3 tablespoons flower water
1 cup syrup

Syrup:

Ingredients:
3 cups sugar
1 ½ cup water
2 tablespoons flower water
1 tablespoon lemon juice

Method:
1. Combine milk, corn flour and sugar in a large pan. Stir frequently until thick and bubbly.
2. Add gum crushed with little sugar and flower water. Pour into deep oven dish. Sprinkle with bread crumbs. Bake in hot oven until lightly golden.
3. Remove from heat. Cool and refrigerate. Slice and drizzle with syrup.

Method:
Boil sugar and water until it bubbles. Add lemon juice. Simmer for 5 minutes. Remove from heat. Stir in flower water and leave to cool.

Rice Pudding

Ingredients:
6 cups milk
1 cup short grain rice
1 cup sugar
1 1/3 cup water
2 tablespoons rose water
1/8 Arabic gum

Method:
1. Boil rice with water in medium pan until soft and most of water has evaporated.
2. Add milk and sugar. Simmer on low heat. Stir occasionally for an hour. Remove from heat .Stir rose water and crushed Arabic gum with little sugar.
3. Spoon in small serving bowls. Refrigerate and serve cold.

Barley Milk Pudding

Ingredients:
1 cup boiled barley and soft
5 cups milk
3 tablespoons corn flour
1/3 cup water
8 to 10 tablespoons sugar
2 tablespoons flower water
¼ cup pine nut
¼ cup pistachio
¼ cup almonds

Method:
1. Add milk and barley in a large pan. Simmer on low heat. Stir corn flour mixed with water. Stir until it slightly thickens.
2. Remove from heat. Stir flower water, almonds, pistachio and pine nut. Pour into small serving bowls. Refrigerate and serve cold.

SWEETS

Layali Lebnan

Ingredients:
1 cup fine semolina
6 cups milk
1/3 teaspoon Arabic gum
2 cups fresh whipped cream
1 can thick cream
Crushed pistachio

Method:
1. Combine semolina and milk in a medium pan on low heat. Stir until thick. Remove from heat. Crush Arabic gum with a bit of sugar. Stir with semolina mixture.
2. Pour into a serving plate. Cool.
3. Serve sliced, drizzled with syrup.

Note: It is optional to add sliced bananas on top with toasted pine nuts and flaked almonds.
Spread whipped cream evenly on top.
Sprinkle with pistachio.

Sounounia

Ingredients:
1 ½ cups boiled and soft barley
1 ½ cups sugar
¾ cup flower water
¾ cup walnut soaked in water
¾ flaked Almonds soaked in water
¾ cup pine nuts soaked in water
1 cup fresh pomegranate

Method:
1. Combine barley and sugar in a large pan. Stir on low heat for 5 minutes.
2. Remove from heat. Stir flower water.
3. Chop walnut, almond, pine nut and pomegranate. Stir well. Serve warm in a small bowl.

Semolina Cheese Halawah

Ingredients:
2 cups fine semolina (Firkha)
1 cup sugar
½ a cup unsalted butter
4 ½ cups water
1 tablespoon lemon juice
250g Akawi sweetened cheese or mozzarella
Almonds and pine nuts

Method:
1. Combine semolina and butter in a medium pan on low heat. Stir until semolina changes in color.
2. Boil sugar and water until boiling. Add lemon juice and simmer for 5 minutes.
3. Add syrup with semolina. Stir well. Add chopped cheese. Mix well to combine.
4. Pour into a deep serving plate. Sprinkle with almonds and pine nuts. Serve hot.

EM Ali Pudding

Ingredients:
500g baked puff pastry
4 cups milk
2 cans thick cream
¾ cup sugar
1 teaspoon vanilla essence
1/3 cup pistachio
1/3 cup almonds
1/3 cup raisins
Sprinkle shredded coconut

Method:
1. Crush baked pastry in a deep oven dish. Sprinkle nuts evenly.
2. Boil milk, sugar and vanilla in a small pan. Add cream. Stir well.
3. Pour milk over pastry. Let stand for 1 hour.
4. Bake in hot oven until slightly golden top. Serve it hot.

Halwet Al Jibneh

Ingredients:
1 kg shredded mozzarella cheese
1 cup milk
½ a cup sugar
1 cup fine semolina (firkha)
Rose water

Syrup:

Ingredients:
3 cups sugar
1 ½ cup water
1 tablespoon lemon juice
1 tablespoon flower water

Method:
Boil sugar and water in a small pan until it bubbles. Add lemon juice and boil for 5 minutes. Remove from heat stir flower. Cool.

Method:
1. Add milk and sugar in a large pan on heat until sugar dissolves. Stir with semolina and cheese. Stir upwards pulling the dough until it turns into one ball. Remove from heat.
2. Spread syrup on kitchen table. Pour the cheese mixture and roll to a thin dough then leave aside to cool.
3. Sprinkle rose water evenly on the dough. Shred it to large pieces.
4. Add some syrup and rose water in a container. Put cheese and cover. Refrigerate.
5. Serve in a small plate with drizzled syrup and some Ashta (Ref. pg 288) on the side.

Almond Halwah

Ingredients:
250g ground Almonds
1 cup icing sugar
1 drop flower water
¼ cup sliced pistachio

Method:
1. Combine almond, icing sugar, flower water. Stir to a firm dough.
2. Divide dough.
3. Roll ½ a teaspoon of fruit shape place and slice pistachio on top. Dip in caster sugar and serve.

Custard Biscuit

Ingredients:
200g plain biscuit
4 cups custard
4 sliced bananas
2 cups thick whipped cream
2 tablespoons unsalted butter

Method:
1. Crush biscuits well. Mix with butter. Spread evenly on a serving plate. Pour custard to cover.
2. Cool well. Evenly spoon cream on top. Arrange banana on top cool. Slice to serve.

Namourah

Ingredients:
1 ¼ cup yoghurt
2 cups sugar
½ a cup ghee
½ a cup shredded coconut
1 teaspoon carbonate of soda
1/3 cup pine nuts
4 tablespoons flower water
4 tablespoons rose water

Method:
1. Combine all the ingredients except for pine nuts. Stir well to a soft batter.
2. Brush a deep oven tray with Tahini paste. Cover well. Pour batter in. Sprinkle with pine nuts, leave to rest for 2 hours.
3. Bake in a hot oven until golden brown. Remove from heat. Pour cold syrup and cool in the tray.
4. Cut to Medium Square and serve.

Syrup:

Ingredients:
3 cups sugar
1¼ cup water
1 tablespoon flower water
½ a teaspoon Arabic gum
1 tablespoon lemon juice
½ a tablespoon ghee

Method:
Boil sugar and water until it bubbles. Add lemon juice and boil for 5 minutes. Remove from heat. Add crushed Arabic gum with little sugar and ghee.

Basama

Ingredients:
4 cups semolina
2 cups flour
2 cups melted ghee
2 cups sugar
3 cups water

Method:
Combine all ingredients to soft dough almost like breadcrumbs.

Filling:

Ingredients:
½ a cup finely crushed pistachio
½ a cup pine nuts
½ a cup sugar
1 ¼ cup cashew nuts finely crushed
1 teaspoon ghee

Syrup:

Ingredients:
3 cups sugar
¾ cup water
1 tablespoon lemon juice
1 tablespoon rose water
1 tablespoon flower water

Method:
Boil sugar and water. Add lemon juice. Boil for 3minutes. Remove from heat. Stir rose and flower water. Cool.

Method:
1. Divide dough in half. Press half in a deep oven tray well. Take cashew nuts mixed with sugar and ghee. Press well evenly.
2. Spoon pistachio on top of cashew. Press well as well as the pine nut. Add the second half of dough, evenly pressing well to coat. Bake in hot oven until golden brown. Pour syrup evenly on top and sprinkle some crushed pistachio.
3. Cool in the tray. Slice to squares to serve.

Zalabiah

Ingredients:
3 cups plain flour
1 teaspoon baking powder
¼ cup oil
1 teaspoon instant yeast
2 tablespoons anise powder
2 tablespoons mahaleb
1 tablespoon daat kack
1 tablespoon vanilla
Sprinkle of salt

Method:
1. Combine all ingredients in a large bowl, adding water gradually to soft sticky dough. Cover to double in size.
2. Heat oil in a deep frying pan.
3. Dip your hands in water and pull a piece of dough.
4. Stretch thinly with the hands deep fry until golden brown. Drain on kitchen towel.
5. Serve dipped in syrup or sprinkle with icing sugar.

Syrup:

Ingredients:
3 cups sugar
1 ½ cup water
1 tablespoon lemon juice
1 tablespoon lemon juice
1 tablespoon flower water

Method:
Boil sugar and water until it bubbles. Add lemon juice boil for 5 minutes. Remove from heat. Stir flower water.

Knefe

Ingredients:
1 kg fine knefe
227g soft butter
½ a kg shredded mozzarella cheese
8 cups water
12 tablespoons milk powder
2 cups sugar
2 cups fine semolina
½ a cup flower water
½ a cup rose water

Method:
1. Combine semolina and butter. Knead to a soft sough. Divide dough in half. Evenly press into medium oven tray. Bake until the sides turn gold and remove from oven. Sprinkle cheese evenly.
2. Stir in water, milk, sugar and semolina in a medium pan. Stir frequently until thick. Remove from heat. Add flower water, rose water and stir well. Pour over cheese evenly to cover and leave aside to cool.
3. Bake in the oven until it bubbles. Slowly remove. Cut to squares in a serving plate and add on top of a drizzle of syrup. Serve it hot with the dough side up.

Sufouf

Ingredients:
2 cups plain flour
2 cups fine semolina
2 ½ cups sugar
2 cups water
1 cup oil
3 teaspoons baking powder
4 tablespoons ground anise
4 tablespoons ground turmeric
1 teaspoon sesame seeds

Method:
1. Combine all the ingredients in a large bowl, except the sesame seed. Stir well with a wooden spoon.
2. Brush a deep oven tray with Tahini paste and coat well.
3. Pour mixture. Sprinkle with sesame seeds. Let to rest for 30 minutes.
4. Bake in hot oven until golden brown. Cool in the tray slice to square and serve.

Awaymat Duns

Ingredients:
2 cups plain flour
1 teaspoon instant yeast
1 small boiled potato
¼ cup flower water
3 cups syrup

Method:
1. Mash the potato and put in strainer over a bowl. Gradually add 1 to 1 ½ cups water. Stir until potato done. Reserve the juice.
2. Combine flour, yeast and flower water with potato. Juice whisking to medium stick dough. Leave to rest and double in size.
3. Heat oil in a deep pan. Dip a teaspoon in water and take an amount of dough and fry until golden brown. Remove with a slotted spoon. Stir in syrup for 1 minute. Serve hot or cold.

Syrup:

Ingredients:
3 cups water
1 ½ cups water
1 tablespoon lemon juice
1 tablespoon flower water

Method:
1. Boil until it bubbles.
2. Add lemon juice, boil for 5 minutes, remove from heat.
3. Stir flower water.

Meshabak

Ingredients:
2 cups corn flour
1 ½ cup plain yoghurt
¼ cup plain flour
2 cups syrup
1 teaspoon baking powder
Sprinkle of Saffron

Method:
1. Combine all ingredients well to soft dough in a bowl cover. Leave to rest for 10 minutes.
2. Place dough in piping bag or a cone with small hole.
3. Heat oil in a deep pan and drizzle over the oil in 2 circles over each other until lightly golden. Remove with a slotted spoon. Stir in syrup for 1 minute. Serve hot or cold.

Othmaliya

Ingredients:
3 ½ cups milk
1 cup sugar
½ a cup fine semolina
1 tablespoon heaped corn flour
85g thick cream
1 tablespoon rose water
1 tablespoon flower water
250g knefe vermicelli
2 cups syrup

Method:
1. Combine milk, sugar, semolina and corn flour in a medium pan on low heat. Stir frequently until thick. Remove from heat and stir in cream and water.
2. Pour on flat serving plate and leave aside to cool.
3. Toast knefe vermicelli in the oven until golden brown. Remove from oven. Sprinkle over cream evenly.
4. Patter vermicelli with ground pistachio into medium squares and add 1 teaspoon of cream in the center of the square.
5. Serve sliced and drizzled with syrup.

Ladies' Fingers (Zounoud Al Sit)

Ingredients:
1 packet filo pastry
4 cups Ashta (Ref. pg 288)
2 cups syrup (Ref. pg 311)
1 cup ground pistachio

Method:
1. Cut pastry to 10 cm long then in half. Put it over each other like a cross to be centered.
2. Add 1 tablespoon of Ashta in the center. Fold well the sides. Roll the rest. Seal well to prevent the Ashta from leaking.
3. Heat oil in a large pan. Fry rolls until golden brown. Drain in kitchen towel.
4. Dip each roll in cold syrup. Line them in a serving plate sprinkled with pistachio.

Mafrouke

Ingredients:
500g fine semolina
1 tablespoon ghee
½ a cup syrup
500g fresh cream
(Ashtah. Ref. pg 288)
2 tablespoons grounded pistachio
1 ½ cups sugar
¼ cup flower water
¼ cup rose water

Method:
1. Combine semolina, ghee and sugar on low heat. Stir frequently until golden brown.
2. Add syrup and water. Stir well to a sticky dough. Remove from heat. Leave to rest for 40 minutes. If it is hard, stir 2 cups of water without heat.
3. Spoon on serving plate. Flatten slightly with the back of spoon and leave aside to cool.
4. Spoon Ashtah evenly on the dough. Sprinkle with pistachio. Serve sliced.

Attaief

Ingredients:
1 ½ cup plain flour
3 tablespoons sugar
2 teaspoons baking powder
½ a teaspoon instant yeast
¼ cup flower water
2 ¼ cups water

Method:
1. Combine all the ingredients to thick liquid dough in a bowl. Cover to double in size, whisking occasionally.
2. Brush a large frying pan with oil. Heat on fire. Spoon 3 tablespoons of mixture to make small rounds.
3. Until lightly golden, remove from pan. Place on a tray cover with towel until done.

Filling:

Ingredients:
3 cups water
½ a cup fine semolina
12 tablespoons milk powder
225g thick cream
(Ashtah. Ref. pg 288)

Method:
1. Combine all ingredients in a pan on medium heat, stirring frequently until it bubbles and thick. Remove from heat and leave aside to cool.
2. Spoon 1 tablespoon of filling in center of Attaief. Press one side well to seal. Line them in a serving plate. Sprinkle ground pistachio on top of cream. Serve drizzled with syrup.

Hint:
Fill crushed walnuts mixed with sugar and rose water. Take 1 tablespoon in the center of dough. Seal well and deep fry in hot oil or bake in an oven. Dip in syrup while hot.

Simple Cake

Ingredients:
5 eggs
1 ½ teaspoons vanilla essence
2 ¼ cups plain flour
227g unsalted butter
1 cup milk
1 teaspoon baking powder
1 ½ cups sugar

Method:
1. Grease deep 25 cm round cake pan.
2. Combine sugar, eggs and vanilla essence in medium bowl of electric mixer. Beat until mixture changes in color. Add butter mix well.
3. Add stiffed flour, baking powder and milk. Beat on medium speed until all ingredients are combined smooth and changed in color.
4. Spread mixture into prepared pan. Bake in moderate oven for about 45 to 50 minutes. Stand 5 minutes before turning on to wire rack to cool.

Hint: Replace ¼ cup of flour with cocoa for a simple chocolate cake.

SWEETS

Carrot and Pineapple Cake

Ingredients:
2 cups plain flour
1 ½ cups sugar
1 cup oil
4 eggs
2 cups grated carrots
1 teaspoon vanilla essence
1 small can chopped pineapple
2 teaspoons baking powder
½ a teaspoon carbonate of soda
½ a cup crushed walnuts
Sprinkle of salt

Method:
1. Grease seep 30 cm of pan cake.
2 Combine oil and sugar in a bowl of electric mixer. Beat well. Add eggs, vanilla and beat until light and smooth.
3. Sift flour, baking powder and soda. Add ¾ of the mixture to the egg mixture. Beat until well combined.
4. Stir in a small bowl carrot, pineapple and ¼ of the flour mix well to coat.
5. Add to the mixture and fold with the spoon. Spread into prepared pan. Bake in moderate oven about 45 to 50 minutes. Stand for 5minutes before turning to wire rack to cool.

Date Cake

Ingredients:
4 eggs
2 cups plain flour
4 teaspoons baking powder
250g seeded dates
Lemon zest or orange zest
1 ½ teaspoons ground cinnamon
1 ½ teaspoons ground nutmeg
1/3 cup ghee
1 cup milk
1 cup sugar
1 ½ cups vanilla essence

Method:
1. Grease deep 30cm round cake pan.
2. Combine sugar, eggs and vanilla in medium bowl of electric mixer. Beat until smooth and creamy. Add ghee, zest and beat until change in color.
3. Add sifted flour with spices, baking powder and milk. Beat on medium speed until all ingredients are well combined.
4. Add dates and walnuts. Fold with a spoon. Spread into prepared pan and bake in moderate oven for about 45 minutes. Stand for 5minutes before turning to wire rack to cool.

Truffle Cake

Ingredients:
½ a sliced simple cake
1 cup orange juice
3 cups custard
1 can mixed fruits
1 packet orange Jell-o
2 cups whipped cream

Method:
1. Press half the cake in a 25cm spring form tin. Drizzle with orange juice and spread custard evenly.
2. Spread fruit all over custard. Cool in refrigerator. Pour Jell-o mixture. Refrigerate until firm.
3. Spread cream all over. Remove from tin. Place in a serving plate.

Note: Custard

Ingredients:
3 cups milk
5 tablespoons sugar
2 ½ tablespoons custard powder

Ingredients:
Combine all in a medium pan on medium heat, stirring frequently until it thickens and bubble.

Jell-o

Follow the instructions on the packet

Pineapple Cake

Ingredients:
4 eggs
2 cups plain flour
2 cups sugar
2 teaspoons baking powder
1 teaspoon vanilla
400g canned whole pineapple

Method:
1. Strain pineapple over a small bowl. Reserve the juice.
2. Add 4 tablespoons of sugar in a deep 25cm cake pan on low heat until it caramelizes. Spread evenly. Place pineapple rings all over.
3. Combine eggs, sugar and vanilla in a medium bowl. Beat with electric mixer until light and change in color.
4. Add reserved juice and the sifted flour with baking powder until well combined.
5. Spread the mixture over the pineapple rings. Bake in moderate oven for 30 to 45 minutes. Remove from oven and pour evenly 1 cup of pineapple juice. Leave to cool in the pan and turn it on serving plate to serve.

Almond Apple Cake

Ingredients:
3 peeled and sliced apples
5 eggs
1 cup sugar
1 cup plain flour
117g unsalted butter
1 teaspoon baking powder
1 teaspoon vanilla essence
1/4 cup toasted almonds
1 tablespoon icing sugar
Sprinkle of cinnamon

Method:
1. Grease deep 30 cm cake pan.
2. Line apples in the pan. Sprinkle almonds, icing sugar and cinnamon.
3. Combine eggs, sugar and vanilla essence in a medium bowl of electric mixer. Beat until mixture is smooth. Add butter and beat on medium speed until mixture change in color.
4. Add sifted flour, baking powder to mixture. Beat until well combined.
5. Spread into pan over the apple. Bake in moderate oven about 45 minutes. Stand for 5 minutes before turning to serving plate and leave aside to cool.

Apple Cake

Ingredients:
2 cups plain flour
1 cup oil
2 cups sugar
5 eggs
1 teaspoon vanilla
1 teaspoon baking powder
1 teaspoon carbonate of soda
Sprinkle of salt
2 teaspoons cinnamon powder
1 cup crushed walnuts
4 apples cut into cubes

Method:
1. Grease deep 30 cm cake pan.
2. Combine eggs, sugar and vanilla in medium bowl of electric mixer. Beat until change in color. Add oil beat until smooth.
3. Add sifted flour, baking powder, soda and spices to the mixture. Beat well until combined.
4. Add apples and walnut to the mixture. Fold with a spoon. Spread in prepared pan. Bake in moderate oven about 45 to 50 minutes. Stand for 5 minutes before turning on wire rack to cool.

Banana Cake

Step 1

Ingredients:
2 ½ cups plain flour
1 teaspoon baking powder
¾ teaspoon carbonate of soda
½ a teaspoon salt

Method:
Sift all ingredients in a large bowl.

Step 2

Ingredients:
2 eggs
1 ½ cups sugar
½ a cup unsalted butter

Method:
Combine all in medium bowl of electric mixer until change in color and smooth.

Step 3

Ingredients:
4 ripe bananas
1 teaspoon vanilla essence
1 ¾ cup plain yoghurt

Method:
Mash bananas in a small bowl mix with vanilla and yoghurt.

Step 4

Combine all steps. Mix well until smooth spread in a deep 30cm greased pan. Bake in moderate oven about 45 to 50 minutes. Stand 5 minutes before turning on wire rack to cool. Dust icing sugar on top before serving.

Fruit Cake

Ingredients:
1 ½ cup plain flour
1 cup sugar
½ a cup milk
3 eggs
1 teaspoon vanilla
Lemon zest
112g soft unsalted butter
2 tablespoons ghee
3 teaspoons baking powder
½ a teaspoon ground nutmeg
½ a teaspoon cinnamon powder
200g mixed dry fruits

Method:
1. Grease 18cm * 25cm loaf pan.
2. Combine butter, ghee and sugar in medium bowl of electric mixer until smooth.
3. Add eggs, vanilla beat well until light and change in color.
4. Add sifted flour, spices and baking powder. Mix well with milk until well combined.
5. Fold mixed dry fruits spread in loaf pan. Bake in moderate oven for 35 to 45 minutes. Stand 5 minutes before turning on wire rack to cool.

Chocolate Cake

Ingredients:
6 eggs
2 cups plain flour
2 cups sugar
1 cup cocoa
112g butter soft
3 tablespoons ghee
1 ½ teaspoons vanilla
Lemon zest
1 cup milk
3 teaspoons baking powder

Method:
1. Grease 30cm cake pan.
2. Combine sugar, eggs and vanilla rest in medium bowl of electric mixer until change in color.
3. Add butter and ghee beat until combined, stir in sifted flour, cocoa, baking powder. Beat well and add milk. Beat to a smooth batter.
4. Spread in pan. Bake in moderate oven for 45 to 55 minutes. Stand 5 minutes before turning on wire rack to cool.

Need's Chocolate Cake

Ingredients:
6 eggs
1 cup sugar
¾ cup plain flour
2 teaspoons baking powder
1 teaspoon vanilla essence
¼ cup cocoa

Sauce:

Ingredients:
1 ½ cups water
4 tablespoons sugar
4 tablespoons cocoa

Method:
Combine in a small saucepan on low heat until sugar dissolves. Remove from heat.

Cream:

Ingredients:
500g drinking cocoa
340g cream (or 3 cans of cream)

Combine in a small bowl and stir until thick.

Method:
1. Grease a deep 20 cm round cake container.
2. Combine sugar, eggs and vanilla in the medium bowl of an electric mixer. Blend until color changes.
3. Add sifted flour, cocoa, baking powder and beat until combined. Spread in pan, bake in moderate oven for 30 to 40 minutes. Stand 5 minutes before turning on serving plate then cool aside.
4. Split cake in half and spread sauce evenly on both sides. Spread a cup of cream evenly on the base. Cover top with the top layer and spread rest of cream over the cake.
5. Refrigerate well before serving.

Coconut Cake

Ingredients:
5 eggs
1 cup milk
2 cups plain flour
2 cups sugar
117g unsalted butter
Lemon zest
1 teaspoon vanilla essence
3 teaspoons baking powder
1 cup shredded coconut
½ a cup tasted flaked almonds
½ a cup apricot jam

Method:
1. Grease deep 30cm round cake pan.
2. Combine eggs, sugar, vanilla and zest in medium electric mixer bowl until the color changes. Add butter and beat well.
3. Add sifted flour, baking powder, coconut and milk beat until combined and smooth.
4. Spread in pan, bake in moderate oven for 45 minutes and stand 5 minutes before turning on wire rack to cool.
5. Place cake on serving plate. Spread ½ a cup of apricot jam on top evenly. Sprinkle almonds and serve.

Eggless Cake

Ingredients:
2 ½ cups plain flour
1 ½ cups sugar
½ a cup oil
1 ½ cups orange juice
½ a cup shredded coconut
3 teaspoons baking powder
1 tablespoon Tahini paste
½ a cup apricot jam
3 tablespoons shredded coconut extra

Method:
1. Brush Tahini paste in a deep 25cm round cake pan. Combine sifted flour, sugar, oil, juice, coconut and baking powder in an electric mixer bowl. Beat until ingredients are combined and smooth. Pour mixture in prepared pan and bake in moderate oven for 30 to 35 minutes. Stand in pan until cool.
2. Turn over a plate. Spread jam evenly, sprinkled with coconut.

Arabic Ice Cream

Ingredients:
1 kg fresh milk
8 tablespoons icing sugar
8 tablespoons instant Sahlab
1 teaspoon Arabic gum crushed with Sprinkle of sugar

Method:
1. Combine all the dry ingredients in a large pan. Add milk stirring frequently on medium heat until thick bubbly cream is formed. Remove from heat.
2. Pour into 2 lamington pans. Refrigerate to cool. Remove from refrigerator and beat well. Add the flavoring. Beat until combined then freeze.
3. Repeat beating process once more then freeze until firm.

Flavorings:

1. Blend strawberries or raspberries and add to cream. Mix well.
2. Toast almonds. Melt 2 tablespoons of sugar in the pan until caramelized. Mix with almonds. Cool the mix with cream.
3. Fresh Pistachio crushed mixed with cream.
4. Cocoa or melted chocolate mixed with cream.

Cheesecake

Ingredients:
250g digestive biscuit
50g unsalted butter at room temperature
4 tablespoons sugar
400g creamy cheese at room temperature
¾ cup sugar
4 tablespoons gelatin
¼ cup hot water
2 white eggs at room temperature
510 g thick cream or 3 cans cream (170g each)

Method:
Mix biscuit, butter and 4 tablespoons of sugar in a blender to a smooth crust, Press it into the bottom of the pan into an even layer.
Beat the creamy cheese and sugar well using an electric mixer. Dissolve the gelatin in hot water and add to mixture. Beat well.
Whisk egg whites until thick and fluffy fold in the cream.
Combine with cheese mixture by folding. Do not over mix.
Pour creamy cheese filling into the prepared pan. Place it in the refrigerator to cool and for it to maintain its shape.

Topping:

Any kind of your choice: Cherry, strawberry, blueberry can (595g) Mix one can with 5 tablespoons of icing sugar ,spread over cheese cake and leave it to cool until serving time.

How To...

- Chocolate's healing powers
- Foods to boost your brain
- How fruits and vegetables can change your life
- How organic is the new trend?
- How to ace the perfect Mediterranean table set up
- How to prepare a last minute dinner party
- How to rock the perfect low budget dinner party
- Romantic ways to use food
- The 10 must-know cooking techniques
- The power of rice
- The right wines for the right foods
- Why this book is your best friend

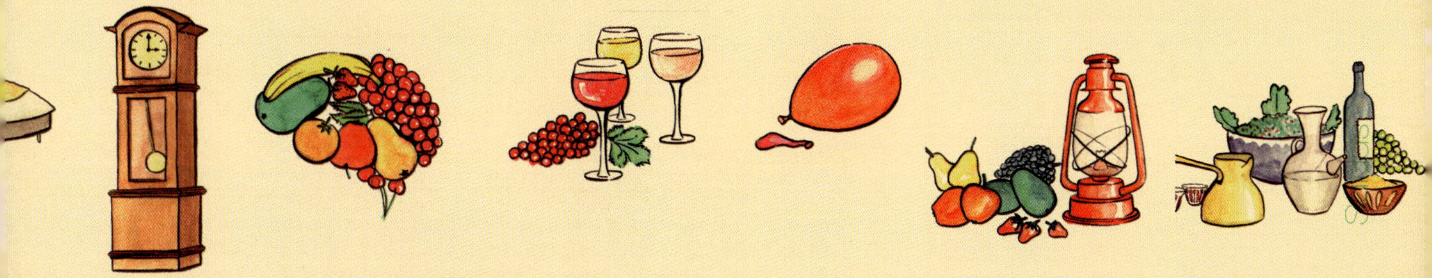

How To...

Chocolate's healing powers

"Life is like a box of chocolate... you never know what you might get."

You never know what life has hidden for you. Some of its surprises are good and others... not so much. But we all know that you can't change what is beyond your control; so how about starting with what you can improve: your health. Dietitians already covered the "one apple a day keeps the doctor away" part. The trainers have also done a great job convincing you that exercising is the best solution to losing weight and improving your health. Those solutions are sometimes hard to follow, so how about a cure that is a bit sweeter to digest...

Chocolate has literally become the cure of a "broken heart"; it actually lowers the risk of heart diseases, diabetes, even obesity, and also regulates your blood pressure. Got your attention so far? And for all of you women out there, know that chocolate in moderation actually delays the aging process because it contains antioxidants that have direct effect on aging. Interested enough? How about knowing that chocolate reduces stress and decreases your chances of feeling down and constantly tired...It gives you energy and helps regulating your hormones... Convinced? I guess that's a yes!

In the end moderation is the key. Chocolate is no longer the cure for the heartbroken or single people not ready to mingle yet... It's for everyone; and remember, the darker the chocolate the brighter your days will be.

Foods to boost your brain

If you're interested in improving your memory - and let's face it, who isn't – there is indeed a way to make that happen.

Whether you're improving your ability to remember names, your mother's birthday or crucial facts you need for a job interview, keeping your brain in tiptop shape should be high on your agenda. Dietary choices play a major role in your brain's functioning: proper nutrition keeps it working to its fullest, protects its cells and helps it work efficiently and effectively.

Here are some of the finest brain boosters, recommended by the experts:

Blackberries – Not the phones - Whether it's a new dance or a foreign language, the older you get the harder it is to learn new things.

Blackberries can get the conversation flowing again. They provide potent antioxidants known as polyphenols, improving our ability to soak up new information.

Coffee - A recent Finnish study reveals that people who sipped between three to five cups of coffee a day in their 40s and 50s reduced their odds of developing Alzheimer's disease by 65 percent compared with those who downed fewer than two cups a day.

Apples - Here's a new reason to munch on an apple a day: Apples are a leading source of quercetin, an antioxidant plant chemical that keeps your mental juices flowing by protecting your brain cells.

Chocolate - You've definitely heard the good news that chocolate can lower your blood pressure helping protect against age-related memory loss.

Spinach - This leafy green is packed with nutrients that prevent dementia like vitamin E and vitamin K.

Salmon - This swimmer isn't just good for your ticker, it's good for your grey matter too. Salmon is a top source of DHA, the predominant omega-3 fat in your brain, believed to protect against Alzheimer's disease.

Maintaining a good level of these foods in your diet gives a comforting insurance of balanced and solid health but most importantly an efficient stimulant for your brain. And trust me, we all need that!

How To...

How fruits and vegetables can change your life

For all those who think that fruits and vegetables are a cliché, old fashioned, and abused culinary topic... think again. Just like you can't judge people, it is not acceptable to judge fruits and vegetables. You underestimate their power; therefore, it is a must to enlighten your views about them.

As corny as it may sound, think of these two components as the colors of a rainbow: each color focuses on building the immunity system in its own way.

Green foods such as broccoli, kale, romaine lettuce, spinach and cabbage help the circulatory system. Red foods like tomatoes and watermelon help protect the skin especially from the sun's effect.

For something a bit brighter, Orange foods like carrots, pumpkins, squash, sweet potatoes, and apricots help protect the DNA and provide the different vitamins to your system.

Now if you're feeling a bit rusty, the Green and Yellow foods such as yellow corn, green peas, avocado and honeydew melon will give you a bit more strength to the bones. As for the Orange and Yellow foods, they prevent inflammation and heart disease and that includes oranges, pineapple, tangerines, peaches and papaya. And finally the Red, Blue and Purple fruits and vegetables are powerful antioxidants... meaning: less wrinkles and joint pain.

So instead of sitting all day like in a comfortable couch texting on your blackberry, how about focusing on having a share of blueberries, strawberries, cranberries and blackberries every now and then. Just like after every rain, there's a rainbow, consider the following: after every bag of chips, an apple awaits!

How organic is the new trend?

There is nothing more depressing than accepting the fact that you are simply "unique.... Yet just like everyone else." You want to follow the latest trends in fashion and style, but what about your own health and metabolism?

Here's the catch!

Being organic is no longer a phase that people go through, rather a lifestyle. People get to know it, define it, accept it and live by it. Nonetheless, just like not everyone can afford Gucci, Prada or Givenchy, not everyone can afford going 100% organic.

Bottom line, here are some healthy and accessible alternatives for your food!

The 1st step in this process is to believe that you can do it... it is not about starving yourself to death nor spending the day at the gym checking the pounds dripping off of you, it's a about a choice you make, but mostly the commitment to not altering your new gained habits.

The 2nd step is to start shifting with the additives of your meals, such as fruits. For instance, when it comes to apples and peaches forty-five different pesticides and chemicals are being applied to them.... can't find organic? Then how about watermelon, tangerines, oranges, grapefruits and bananas? Blueberries, kiwis and raspberries and so many others, can replace grapes.

The 3rd step is acknowledging the fact that this change is a long-term commitment, just like everything in life.

And remember, what comes easily, goes away easily! So hang on in there and you'll just love the results.

How To...

How to ace the perfect Mediterranean table set up

You're on the wrong track when you convince yourself that spending the day in the kitchen is a bliss. Your back starts to hurt you, you lose feeling of your legs and you end up chopping your fingers with the veggies of your salad. Then comes the moment where your table is all set. You are so proud of your work. You dedicate the final minutes to your final touches. The dressing: perfect. The oven: checked. You sit at the table after gathering the family and the food has never smelled so good. One hour later, it's time to wash the dishes. You haven't enjoyed the food that you spent hours preparing, or the laughter of your kids. That is why the Mediterranean feast and specifically the Meza combine good food and good time all around the same table.

The Mediterranean table is by far one of the most appealing to the eye and stomach. It's the perfect match between the homemade dishes and the family spirit. You can enjoy barbecuing while hanging out with your family outside. There's nothing better than holding a glass of Araa', which is the must-have drink in the Meza, and toasting on good health and great times.

To prepare the food, the first thing to do is be ready for diversity. It is not a matter of salad, meat, and cake; it is about the delicious Fattoush and Tabbouleh in the beginning, followed by Mutabbal or Babaghanoush (eggplant), Hummus, Kibbeh, Shanklish and Spicy lamb and beef sausages also known as Maqaniq and Sujuk. Just talking about it makes you wish that Sundays would come faster! As for the garnishing, believe it or not, a huge bowl of vegetables in the middle of your table will do the trick; use onions, cucumbers, tomatoes, mint and feel free to let your senses go wild!

And of course, no matter how full you are, you must leave room for the perfect dessert. Some people are satisfied with fresh fruits, yet others are still a bit more daring and wouldn't mind some cream and honey, some sorbet, or maybe a bit of Knefe.

Remember that when it comes to the Meza, no matter how overwhelming you might think the preparation is, you won't feel the hard work because you'll be surrounded by your friends and family.

Great food! Great drinks! And the best people! Couldn't ask for more, right?

How to prepare a last minute dinner party

You wake up in the morning. Off you take that usual rushed shower and warm cup of coffee that takes the psychological effect of waking you up... You have a busy day ahead of you; whether it's getting the kids ready for school, heading to work or taking care of the house whole, you've got it all figured out; you're on time and enjoying how talented you've become in your own time management. Your marathon day is about to take its happy end as all your tasks are done and you're finally headed home for a peaceful evening...or not quite: Your day hasn't even begun! It strikes you that you proudly invited friends for dinner.

Well, don't panic, here are a few tips that might release the pressure of racing time and help you go through the night in the smoothest way possible.

First, start by managing your chores. You won't have a single thing done if you don't organize the remaining of your time. Check what you have of available foods in your refrigerator, and make a list of the missing items. This will make shopping a lot easier and faster. Start preparing the food the way you want to serve it. First things first: Crackers, chips and beverages; those will help you gain time in case your guests arrive ahead of time. Step two, appetizers and salads. Don't complicate your life over them; keep them quick and simple. Go for chicken wings, ham and cheese or crab cakes. As for the salad choices, you can always go for the fresh veggies with the perfect balsamic sauce. You're ready to go...

Main course! Remember, it's not Thanksgiving, so don't even consider pulling out a heroic 14-hour-recipe like Turkey or Paella. Go for Lasagna and some potato wedges, or some homemade roast beef: Steam it in the oven and proceed with your dessert meanwhile. A mouthwatering fruit salad! Think rainbows for color and flavor: Use mangoes, bananas, kiwis, apples and even pineapple. In the end, it's all about enjoying your time, and not stressing over it.

Do keep in mind that asking for help is only human and never lose track of time in the whole preparation phase. Worst-case scenario, there's a burger joint round every corner!

HOW TO...

337

How To...

How to rock the perfect low budget dinner party

Entertaining friends and family in your home is a much bigger undertaking than many people realize. While it may seem like a more "low key" option than going out, in reality there are a lot of things that go into a successful dinner party it's no wonder that a host can easily get carried away and spend more money than intended.

So here's the key tip. Keep it small!

You can prevent going overboard by limiting your guest list to a number that will fit comfortably into the space you have.

A good rule of thumb is to only invite as many people as can be seated around the table and if you're determined to have a larger guest list, you might consider skipping dinner in favor of appetizers and cocktails.

Keep it simple!

Avoid the temptation of going all-out gourmet for your dinner party. It's extremely expensive and highly unnecessary. Instead, pull out this cookbook and you're bound to find something that will be both delicious and cost-effective.

A good goal to have is to make your event a reflection of you. You want your guests to feel comfortable and enjoy themselves don't worry about impressing them with fancy caviar or overpriced champagne. Odds are your guests will appreciate a relaxed, well-executed get-together more than a stuffy overrated event. Think delicious appetizers, main courses, sides, desserts and even cocktails.

Another great way to limit the stress of planning and orchestrating a dinner party is to unload some of the responsibility. Consider asking guests to pitch in by bringing an appetizer, dessert or beverage to share. This allows you to focus on the main dish, while ensuring everyone will have something to munch on that they will genuinely enjoy. It's a good idea to coordinate who is bringing what so you don't end up with an unbalanced table, but it will save you a lot of work and money.

As for the display, choose a theme that can be visually represented without a lot of work or extra spending on props. Something like fresh cut flowers and candles to create an enjoyable atmosphere that's both esthetically pleasing and comfortable.

Remember, the goal of your dinner party should be to bring together a group of people you want to spend more time with, and to treat them to delicious food, entertaining conversation and a comfortable, welcoming atmosphere. With a little planning, hosting a no-fuss, inexpensive, but still wildly successful dinner party will be a piece of cake.

Romantic ways to use food

Whoever said that food is the comfort of a lonely heart was wrong. Food is one of life's greatest pleasures and it would be an utter mistake not to share it with the one you love. It is not weird to connect food to one's feelings. Why remember the song two lovers once shared and not their favorite meal together? Why remember a perfume and not the aroma of live cooking on a romantic dinner? Food is not just a comforting element for the broken hearted; it's more of a step closer to your lover.

On your first date you seek to impress your partner by going out for dinner in a fancy restaurant... steak perhaps? You think: "Pricy, classy and delicious. It's just one date; it's not like we're going to see each other again". And then the unexpected happens a month later, as you find yourself on her doorstep holding a box of chocolates and strawberries, finally admitting: "I can't stop thinking about you..." Which screams I really like you- but maybe a bit less than chocolate...

Studies have shown that eating chocolate causes the brain to release endorphins, which make people feel loved.

Then comes the moment of truth: "Has it been a year already? Where should we go out for dinner".

Eventually, if you decide to stay home or go out, nothing says "I love you" more than Pasta and wine. It's not only about the romantic Italian influence; it's more about the intimacy between two people who have been together for a while. Enjoying a cup of red wine and some Pasta is all about sharing who you are and what you are feeling with the one you love the most.

So if steak talks sophistication, strawberries talk playful, chocolate talks coy and sweet while Pasta denotes the language of two people becoming one, the final step remains the best.

The hot bowl of soup...

If you're 90 and freezing in bed, would you go for Oysters? I don't think so... After years of being "blissfully married", it's all about the soup!

The morale: Food is a necessity and love, a must... so go with what your heart tells you to do... or your stomach!

How To...

The 10 must-know cooking techniques

Whether you're a man or a woman; single or married, you either have a sense of orientation in the kitchen or you get lost choosing the right tool to use; it is highly recommended to get familiar with a few cooking techniques. Some of them are easy to catch while others require practice.

Technique #1, stirring. It all begins with baby steps. It is very important to know how to stir correctly while cooking in order to create a homogenous mixture and to alter the thickness of the liquid. It would be best to use a wooden spoon to get between the corners.

Technique #2, poaching. The key is patience, because it requires a longer time. The point of it would be to gently cook food such as eggs, fish, chicken, meat and fruits and vegetables in order to maintain moisture and nutrients within.

Technique #3, grilling. If you are no fan of grilling, leave it to those macho men who enjoy it the most – to get the suntan too.

It is important to pay attention to the marinade and the timing. If women can multitask, men can mostly handle holding a beer while managing a couple of hotdogs on the grill.

Technique #4, roasting. This cooking technique is the "dry heat cooking method". You can roast using an oven, before a fire, or by burying in embers or very hot sand: you can go cave style or kitchen special... let your instincts go wild on this one.

Technique # 5, sauté . From French, it involves the notion of the "jump" because it's about cooking at very high heat without keeping the food sitting too long in the pan. The difference between this technique and pan frying is that technique #6 requires less heat and less ingredient motion in the pan.

Technique # 7 goes together with technique #8: baking and blistering. These two methods are usually used for pastries, cakes and cookies. Both are very relaxing; all you have to do is let the food linger in the oven over dry heat. Once the smell is out, it's time to enjoy perfection. Technique #9, stewing, where meats or chicken slowly simmers in a flavorful liquid. Do consider that this method requires time, attention and patience.

And finally technique # 10: braising. For all those anti-diet fans, this technique is yours: the main ingredient is browned in fat for that sinful pleasure of the most gourmet!

The power of rice

Never underestimate the power of little things. Never underestimate the power of rice; which is a lot like us human beings.

When you spot rice, and at a first glance, you think: Soft and weak. But once you come closer, you realize that just like us, it adapts to change, it is strong and shares its happiness with others.

When two people get married; what's the first thing that hits them right in the face... rice. Rice is used in many cultures to celebrate the unity of newly wed. It is a symbol of life and fertility, which explains the tradition of throwing it during weddings, a true emblem of shared happiness. Second and just like us, rice adapts to climate changes. Did you know that on cooking, rice swells to give at least three times its original weight? Ladies? Does it remind you of something? The swelling, the weight gain... food for the thought!

A third interesting similarity would definitely be the diversity. There are more than 40,000 different varieties of rice and there are over 29,000 grains of rice in one pound of long grain rice. Just as there are more than hundreds and thousands of little characteristics in a human being that makes him different and unique...

All rice grains may look alike and all human beings may look the same... but in the end there's a difference in the core... once you peel the outside layer, the inside is far more interesting.

Bottom line. Rice is healthy while humans are seeking to improve their health.

Combine the two, and there you go... the perfect match!

HOW TO...

341

How To...

The right wines for the right foods

What's all the fuss about?

Why can't we just drink any wine with any food?

We're more than glad to answer that question for you! After elaborate research, it has been said that wine connoisseurs present a very good case for pairing just the right wine, with just the right food.
In theory, wine can enhance the flavor of food or obliterate it! So you must make the choice. Do you want a battle going on in your mouth or do you want a delightful dining experience?

Here are some tips to make it possible for you to be able to pick out a good complimentary wine for a meal, but also to enable you to face that wine section at the grocery store with newfound courage.

It may surprise you, but you may know more than you think, when it comes to pairing wine with food. When it's a chilly night in December, do you reach for a crisp white wine or a deep warm red wine? When you order a white fish, do you prefer light white wine or a dark rich red? Now- it's not that easy, you see there are many white wines that would taste as rich in front of that cozy fire as the heavy warm red.

When pairing wine to food, there are some simple rules you should keep in mind. Think- is the food rich in flavor or is it light flavored and lean? Will the food or condiments that have been added to the food be acidic? Will the food be sweet or salty or spice hot? Wines share all of these taste elements. Depending on the wine, the elements will vary. What you should try to do is to pair these under tone elements with the under tones in any given food. If the pairing is successful the wine will enhance the taste of the food, and the wine itself will shine through with a wonderful flavor of its own.

Foods that are high in content such as meat will coat the tongue with fat. So when choosing a wine, you will want a wine that will cut that fat coating. By cutting through the fat on the tongue, you will not only bring home the flavor of the wine, but the wonderful flavor of the food.
Wines that are high in tannins such as Syrah and Cabernet Sauvignon, will cut the fat. Tannins love protein, and when the wine's tannins come in contact with proteins, they bind to them, and clean the tongue.

Tannins are more pronounced in red wines' than in white wines'.

Let's now consider foods that are of a sourer nature. Foods that would be considered high in acid. Like salad with vinaigrette dressing, or fish with lemon or dishes made with tomato sauce. The rule of thumb when pairing wine to foods that are acidic is, meet acid with acid, thus choosing white wines which by nature hold less tannins but a higher level of acidity, such as Riesling, Sauvignon Blanc and Chenin Blanc.

...And for a punch of royalty, go for Chardonnay or Champagne!

342

Why this book is your best friend

Let's face it. Food is to many the most precious element on this Earth. You wake up, you eat. At 1:00 o'clock, you're amazed, but yes you're hungry. At 16:00 o'clock you're craving that afternoon snack. At 19:00 you even forgot all what you have already eaten during day and you're fixing yourself a gourmet dinner.

Point is, what's not to like?

So by giving in to the fact that food is an irreplaceable constituent of your daily life, you might as well have the best food there is.

Which leads us to the following conclusion, so simple yet so powerful:

Make this book your best friend!

Because there's nothing even comparable to a homemade dish, it's time to take matters on your own – with a little help.

Covering all culinary areas that might trigger your interest while home alone, preparing a dinner party or lunch for the kids, it'll all in here.

And here's the guarantee you all long to hear: Try out a single recipe randomly picked from this book and you'll make the conclusion as for the remaining. After all, passionate cooking is contagious by nature, so here's your chance to embrace that Art!

Spice Glossary

Barbari:

Is an Ethiopian spice used in most of the food (sauces, chicken, etc). It's a mix of ground spices.

Mix well:
5 tablespoons onion powder
5 tablespoons garlic powder
½ a teaspoon cinnamon powder
½ a teaspoon cloves powder
1 ½ tablespoons cardammon
1 tablespoon all spice powder
1 tablespoon coriander powder
1 tablespoon cumin powder
2 tablespoons fenugreek powder
½ a tablespoon nutmeg powder
1 tablespoon black pepper powder
1 tablespoon turmeric powder
2 tablespoons ginger powder
3 tablespoons chilli powder
5 tablespoons sweet paprika

Bizar:

Equal amount of:
Cumin seeds
Cinnamon stick
Whole black pepper
Fennel seeds
Coriander seeds
Chili (optional)
Turmeric

Roast all the seeds for 5 minutes, leave it to cool, grind to a fine powder. (To be used for fish, chicken or meat)

Daa it Kaak:

2 tablespoons anise seeds
2 tablespoons fennel seeds
1 tabespoon nutmeg
2 tablespoons mahlab
½ a teaspoon Arabic gum

Roast all the seeds except the Arabic gum, leave it to cool, grind with gum to a fine powder. (To be used for cookies or sweet dough)

Herbes de Provence:

A blend of dried herbs:
2 tablespoons thyme
1 tablespoon rosemary
2 bay leaves
¼ cup basil
2 tablespoons marjoran
3 tablespoons fennel seeds

Grind to powder. (To be used for potato wedges, pasta or chicken)

Ras al Hanut:

2 tablespoons cardammon seeds
2 sticks of cinnamon
1 tablespoon gloves
1 piece nutmeg
2 chilies
1 tablespoon turmeric
2 tablespoons coriander
2 tablespoons cumin
1 tablespoon black pepper

Roast all the seeds, leave to cool, grind to fine powder. (To be used in couscous and all Maroccan food)

Glossary

- **Ajinomoto:**
Monosodium Glutamate which is used as a flavor enhancer.

- **Anise Seeds:**
A seed with aromatic liquorice flavor.

- **Arabic Gum:**
From an aromatic tree grows in the Middle East, known as mistika(small yellow rounds). Or mistak gum.

- **Awarma:**
Made from meat and fat.

- **Baking Powder:**
A raising agent.

- **Basmati Rice:**
White long grained rice.

- **Bay Leaves:**
Aromatic leaves from the bay laurel tree, used fresh or dry.

- **Barbari:**
Ethiopian spice includes garlic.

- **Bizar:**
Ground Spice of equal amount cumin seeds, cinnamon stick, whole black pepper, fennel seeds, coriander seeds, little red chilies and some turmeric toasted all.

- **Burghul:**
Known as cracked wheat.

- **Ginger Root:**
Ginger is the rhizome of the plant Zingiber officinale, consumed whole as a delicacy, medicine, or spice. It lends its name to its genus and family (Zingiberaceae).

- **Caraway Seeds:**
Have a slight anise flavor, available as seeds or ground form.

- **Cardamom:**
Has an exotic fragrance available in pod seeds or ground form.

- **Chickpeas:**
Known as garbanzos.

- **Cinammon:**
Fragrant bark used as a stick or ground form.

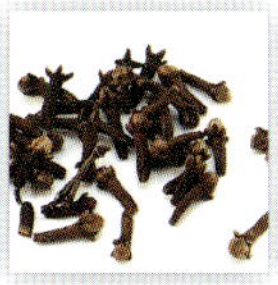

- **Cloves:**
Dried flower buds.

- **Coco Pops:**
Chocolate puffed rice.

- **Coconut:**
Known as desiccated coconut.

- **Corn Flour:**
Starch.

- **Coriander:**
A herb known as cilantro.

- **Couscous:**
A fine cereal made from semolina.

- **Croutons:**
Cutting sliced bread into small cubes and baked.

- **Cumin:**
A spice available as seeds or ground form.

- **Custard Powder:**
Pudding mix.

- **Daa-it-kaak:**
Ground spices of anise seeds, nutmeg-mistaka and mahaleb used for sweets.

- **Eggplant:**
Known as aubergine.

- **Fennel:**
It has an aniseed taste found as seeds or ground form.

- **Five Spice:**
A mixture of ground spices (cinnamon, cloves, fennel, star anise and Szechwan pepper).

- **Garlic:**
An indispensable ingredient in Lebanese cookery.

GLOSSARY

347

- **Ghee:**
Clarified butter.

- **Herbs de Provence:**
An aromatic blend of dried herbs that include thyme, rosemary, bay leaves basil, marjoram and fennel seeds.

- **Hummus:**
A paste of chickpeas, tahini, garlic salt and lemon juice.

- **Jam:**
A preserve of sugar and fruit.

- **Kishik:**
Made from yogurt and cracked wheat.

- **Pomegranate Molasses:**
It is a reduced dark syrup. It is sour flavour to be used for salads, chicken or meat

- **Marsh Mallows:**
Made from sugar, gelatin and corn flour.

- **Marzipan:**
Made from sugar and almonds.

- **Mahlab:**
A spice made of ground black cherry pits, it has a strong fragrant.

- **Milk Powder:**
Made of cow milk.

- **Minced Meat:**
Ground Beef.

- **Mint:**
An aromatic herb.

- **Mixed Spice:**
A blend of all spices.

- **Mograbia:**
Made from semolina similar to couscous but bigger in size.

- **Molasses:**
A thick syrup made from raw sugar.

- **Mozzarella:**
A semi soft cheese that have a melting point.

- **Nutmeg:**
A dried nut of an evergreen tree.

- **Okra:**
Known as bamia, a green ridged oblong pod with furry skin.

- **Molokhia:**
Known as Jute Mallow

- Paprika:
Ground dried red capsicum.

- Pomegranate:
A fruit with leathery red skin with seed juicy flesh.

- Ras Al Hanut:
Moroccan spice made from almost 14 kind of spice.

- Rice Flour:
Flour made from ground rice.

- Rose Water or Flower Water:
Extract made from crushed rose petals used for its aromatic; (saffron) the most expensive spice available in threads, it is made from the dried stamens of the crocus flower.

- Sahlab:
It is ground grain used to thicken sweets used for Arabic ice cream or alone as pudding.

- Semolina:
Made from durum wheat milled into various textured granules.

- Sesame Seeds:
Small seeds harvest from plant. The middle eastern condiment tahini can be substituted for grinding seeds.

- Shallots:
Known as spring onions.

- Soya Sauce:
Made from Soya beans, its salty.

- Stock Cubes:
Available in chicken, vegetables and beef.

- Tahini:
Paste made from crushed sesame seeds.

- Turmeric:
Food coloring from a root of a perennial plant.

- Vanilla Essence:
Vanilla extract.

- Yeast:
Compressed yeast.

- Yoghurt:
Laban.

- Zucchini:
Known as courgette.

- Za'atar:
Mix dry thyme sumac, salt (to powder) add toasted sesone seeds.

GLOSSARY

349

Index

Dips and sauces:

- Avocado dip (p.13)
- Balila (p.13)
- Black olive dip (p.14)
- Cheese dip 1 (p.12)
- Chili sauce (p.19)
- Crab dip (p.18)
- Cucumber dip (p.10)
- Dan's sauce (p.19)
- D.H sauce (p.21)
- Egg and cheese dip (p.14)
- Eggplant dip "babaganouj" (p.15)
- Fava beans "foul medamas" (p.16)
- Garlic dip (p.18)
- Hummus (p.11)
- Ketchup (p.20)
- Mouhamara (p.17)
- Salmon dip (p.11)
- Sweet and sour sauce (p.21)
- Sweet chili sauce (p.20)
- Tomato and avocado dip (p.10)

Salads:

- Avocado salad (p.34)
- Beetroot salad "shamandar" (p.29)
- Broad bean salad (p.35)
- Cabbage salad (p.28)
- Country slaw (p.25)
- Dandelions "hindbeh" (p.45)
- Dan's salad sauce (p.34)
- Egg salad (p.45)
- Fattoush (p.39)
- Feta salad (p.36)
- Green beans salad (p.44)
- Green salad (p.25)
- Grilled salad (p.24)
- Halloumi salad (p.46)
- Hal salad (p.37)
- Mum slaw (p.30)
- Nad salad (p.36)
- Onion salad (p.27)
- Oregano salad (p.43)
- Papaya salad (p.38)
- Pasta salad (p.33)
- Pine nut salad (p.30)
- Potato salad (p.32)
- Raheb (p.47)
- Rice salad (p.42)
- Rocket salad with vegetables (p.26)
- Rocket leaf salad (p.37)
- Silver beet salad (p.44)
- Squid salad (p.38)
- Tabbouleh (p.41)
- Tomato salad (p.28)
- Tuna Macaroni salad (p.31)
- Warm tabbouleh (p.40)
- Yoghurt salad (p.29)

Pickles, jams & chutney:

- Apple jam (p.55)
- Apple jelly (p.58)
- Apple mint chutney (p.61)
- Apricot chutney (p.60)
- Apricot jam (p.54)
- Basic sauce for pickles (p.48)
- Black olives pickles (p.50)
- Capsicum pickles (p.49)
- Carrot pickles (p.49)
- Cauliflower pickles (p.49)
- Cherry jam (p.57)
- Chili pickles (p.51)
- Cucumber pickles (p.49)
- Eggplant makdouse (p.50)
- Eggplant pickles (p.50)
- Fig jam (p.54)
- Fruity jam (p.57)
- Green olives pickles (p.50)
- Mixed vegetables (p.49)
- Nad's chutney (p.60)
- Onion marmalade (p.59)
- Orange marmalade (p.52)
- Quince jam (p.56)
- Quince jelly (p.56)
- Sea weed pickles (p.49)
- Strawberry jam (p.53)
- Sweet chutney (p.61)
- Turnip pickles (p.49)
- Sea weed pickles (p.49)
- Strawberry jam (p.53)
- Sweet chutney (p.61)

350

Dough:

- Almond meat samosa (p.67)
- Baked dough (p.74)
- Basic pizza dough (p.64)
- Brioche (p.80)
- Cheese (p.76)
- Dan's dough (p.71)
- Dough (p.74)
- Falafel (p.89)
- Fatair sabanekh "spinach" (p.66)
- Filling harhara (p.74)
- Fried dough with meat (p.73)
- Grilled dough (p.84)
- Hashwa (p.75)
- Heidi dough (p.81)
- Kishik (p.74)
- Lahim bilajin (p.68)
- Lebanese Bread (p.72)
- Mushroom (p.75)
- Olive bread (p.87)
- Onion rings (p.85)
- Pizza toppings (p.65)
- Safeeha (p.70)
- Saj bread (p.88)
- Salty dough (p.78)
- Salty dough with seasonings (p.79)
- Simple croissant (p.82/83)
- Simple dough (p.72)
- Spring roll dough (p.77)
- Sweet rolls (p.86)
- Vegetable samosa (p.69)
- Za'atar (p.76)

Soups:

- Barley soup (p.104)
- Carrot soup (p.100)
- Chicken soup with rice (p.92)
- Cold soup (p.103)
- Kishek soup (p.101)
- Lentil and potato soup (p.98)
- Meat and vegetables soup (p.95)
- Milk soup (p.97)
- Papaya soup (p.94)
- Pasta lentil soup (p.96)
- Red lentil soup (p.102)
- Special seafood soup (p.99)
- Spinach soup (p.93)
- The easy way for stock preparation (p.105)

Pasta and rice:

- Baked Pasta (p.131)
- Beans moujadara (p.130)
- Chicken biriyani (p.122)
- Chicken rice (p.114)
- Dandi (p.148/149)
- Dry rice (p.109)
- Easy spaghetti (p.142)
- Fettuccine albaha (p.145)
- Fettuccine sausage (p.144)
- Grape leaves and meat (p.128)
- Herbed rice (p.108)
- Lasagne + sauce (p.140/141)
- Linguine meat ball (p.138)
- Machbous cham (p.111)
- Mouhamara "rice" (p.113)
- Paella (p.115)
- Plain rice (p.108)
- Rice and peas (p.124)
- Rice patties (p.129)
- Rice with fish "saiadiat sammak" (p.116)
- Rice with chickpeas (p.110)
- Rice with lentil "masafaieh" (p.121)
- Rice with lentil "midardarah" (p.119)
- Rice with tomato (p.112)
- Rice with vermicelli (p.109)
- Rolled cabbage with rice "malfouf mehshi" (p.123)
- Shells with tuna (p.134)
- Shrimp Biriyani (p.120)
- Spaghetti chili (p.142)
- Spaghetti garlic (p.139)
- Spaghetti tahini (p.139)
- Spaghetti tango (p.135)
- Spaghetti with yoghurt (p.137)
- Spaghetti with zucchini (p.136)
- Spicy sauce/tahini sauce (p.117)
- Tagliatelle cheese (p.147)
- Tagliatelle rishta (p.132)
- Tagliatelle tomato (p.143)
- Tagliatelle with bacon and mushroom (p.133)

INDEX

351

-Tanourine maakroun (p.146)
-Vegetable biriyani (p.118)
-Vegetarian grape leaves (p.126/127)
-Zucchini and eggplant stuffed with rice "maahashi" (p.125)

Vegetarian:

-Altisha (p.174)
-Baked capsicum (p.170)
-Burgul AA banadoura (p.173)
-Dan's couscous (p.157)
-Eggplant with tomato "mousakaa" (p.154)
-Fasoulia bil zeit (p.175)
-Fried eggplant (p.152)
-Koushari (p.153)
-Lubya bil zeit (p.171)
-Mashed potato (p.165)
-Mixed stuffed vegetables (p.169)
-Okra with tomato "bamya" (p.156)
-Pat's potato (p.164)
-Panchit with vegetables (p.162)
-Potato cubes (p.160)
-Potato kibbé (p.158)
-Potato and zucchini (p.163)
-Pumpkin kibbé (p.155)
-Sliced potato "miharaasa" (p.161)
-Sogo (p.176/177)
-Stuffed mushroom (p.166)
-Stuffed tomatoes (p.168)
-Sweet potato (p.167)
-Vegetable stew (p.161)
-Vegetarian burger (p.172)
-Zucchini cakes (p.159)

Sea Food:

-Baby shark and spices (p.183)
-Baked groper (p.182)
-Cham tajin (p.193)
-Cham prawn (p.187)
-Crab with mustard seeds (p.189)
-Fish kibbé (p.194)
-Fish patties (p.181)
-Lobster with cheese (p.191)
-Pan fried fish (p.180)
-Prawn tempura (p.192)
-Spicy fish (p.184)
-Spicy fish with vegetables (p.182)
-Stuffed squid (p.185)
-Squid with ink (p.186)
-Tajin (p.190)
-Tuna burger (p.188)
-Tuna kofta (p.195)

-Tuna with lettuce (p.192)

Poultry:

-Abbzi adoubo (p.208)
-Baked chicken wings (p.207)
-Chicken adobo (p.206)
-Chicken burger (p.204)
-Chicken cordon bleu (p.208)
-Chicken liver (p.209)
-Chicken pancakes (p.202/203)
-Chicken pie (p.199)
-Chicken tikkha (p.201)
-Chicken with honey (p.205)
-Chicken with potato (p.200)
-Shish tawou (p.198)
-Simple roasted chicken (p.200)

Meats:

-Ablama (p.241)
-Aworma (p.253)
-Baked kibbé Dana's (p.250)
-Baked scallops (p.215)
-Bamya with meat "okra" (p.217)
-Beef burger (p.223)
-Beef pastry (p.226)
-Beef with egg (p.245)
-Cham's chili con carne (p.254)
-Dan's burger (p.223)
-Dan's bean steak (p.225)
-Dan's steak (p.216)
-Four types of meatball (p.230/231/232)
-Freekeh (p.237)
-Grilled meat (p.239)
-Habra "raw" (p.236)
-Hareese (p.256)
-Hashwa (p.242)
-Home made sausage (p.243)
-Kafta (p.233/234/235)
-Kebabs (p.239)
-Kibbé habra "raw" (p.236)
-Kibbé with aworma (p.252)
-Kibbé with laban "yoghurt" (p.251)
-Laban emou (p.255)
-Lamb cutlets (p.247)
-Lamb shanks fatteh (p.248)
-Lubieh bil lahm "green beans with meat" (p.224)
-Maklouba (p.214)
-Molokhia "jute mallow" (p.228/229)
-Mougrabia (p.258/259)
-Mustard steak (p.218)
-Pepper steak (p.244)
-Pistachio roast (p.221)

-Potato stew (p.219)
-Roast beef fillet (p.249)
-Roasted lamb legs (p.240)
-Shawarma (p.227)
-Sheikh al meshshi (p.213)
-Shish barak (p.257)
-Spinach with meat (p.222)
-Steak with grape juice (p.220)
-Stuffed artichokes (p.212)
-Stuffed lamb ribs (p.246)
-Veal with cheese (p.255)
-Whole roasted lamb (p.238)

Dairy Products:

-Arisha (p.264)
-Baladi cheese (p.266)
-Dry kishik (p.269)
-Green kishik (p.268)
-Laban "yoghurt" (p.262)
-Labneh (p.263)
-Shami cheese (p.266)
-Shanklish "dry cheese" (p.264)
-Simple cheese (p.265)
-Quick kishik "green kishik"(p.267)
-Zikra cheese (p.266)

Sweets:

-Aish al saraya (p.289)
-Almond apple cake (p.320)
-Almond halwah (p.303)
-Apple cake (p.321)
-Annis biscuits (p.277)
-Arabic ice cream (p.328)
-Ashtah (p.288)
-Ashtalya (p.296)
-Attaief (p.314)
-Awaymat duns (p.309)
-Banana cake (p.322)
-Barley milk pudding (p.297)
-Basama (p.305)
-Butter biscuits (p.280)
-Carrot and pineapple cake (p.316)
-Chocolate cake (p. 324)
-Cheesecake (p.329)
-Cocoa rice (p.295)
-Cocoa spread (p.288)
-Coconut cakes (p.326)
-Coffee pudding (p.290)
-Custard biscuit (p.303)
-Dan's chip biscuits (p.287)
-Date baklawa (p.279)
-Date cake (p.317)

-Date fingers (p.283)
-Date rolls (p.278)
-Dirzi biscuits (p.275)
-Eggless cake (p.327)
-EM Ali pudding (p.301)
-Fruit cake (p.323)
-Ginger biscuits (p.273)
-Gouraiba (p.274)
-Halwet al jibneh (p.302)
-Hibz rice bubbles (p.273)
-Jam biscuits (p.282)
-Jello-O pudding (p.292)
-Kaake zahle (p.276)
-Knefe (p.307)
-Ladies' fingers "zounoud al sit" (p.312)
-Layali lebnan (p.298)
-Mafrouke (p.313)
-Mango pudding (p.294)
-Mehalabia (p.293)
-Meshabak (p.310)
-Milk biscuits (p.281)
-Mini apricot slices (p.285)
-Moughly (p.291)
-Namourah (p.304)
-Need's chocolate cake (p.325)
-Oats biscuits (p.272)
-Othmaliya (p.310)
-Pineapple cake (p.319)
-Pine nut biscuits (p.281)
-Rice flour pudding (p.294)
-Rice pudding (p.297)
-Rock biscuits (p.274)
-Semolina maamoul (p.284)
-Semolina cheese halawah (p.300)
-Semolina halwahh (p.295)
-Simple cake (p.315)
-Sounounia (p.299)
-Sugar biscuits (p.277)
-Sufouf (p.308)
-Sweet macaroon (p.286)
-Truffle cake (p.318)
-Zalabiah (p.306)

Spoons:
1/2Tsp=2.5ml, 1Tps=5ml,
1Dps=10ml, 1Tbsp=15ml

Cups:
1, 1/2, 1/3, 1/4